Why Music Moves Us

WHY MUSIC MOVES US

Jeanette Bicknell

palgrave
macmillan

First published 2009 by
PALGRAVE MACMILLAN

Palgrave Macmillan in the UK is an imprint of Macmillan Publishers Limited,
registered in England, company number 785998, of Houndmills, Basingstoke,
Hampshire RG21 6XS.

Palgrave Macmillan in the US is a division of St Martin's Press LLC,
175 Fifth Avenue, New York, NY 10010.

Palgrave Macmillan is the global academic imprint of the above companies
and has companies and representatives throughout the world.

Palgrave® and Macmillan® are registered trademarks in the United States,
the United Kingdom, Europe and other countries.

ISBN-13: 978-0-230-20989-3 hardback
ISBN-10: 0-230-20989-0 hardback

This book is printed on paper suitable for recycling and made from fully
managed and sustained forest sources. Logging, pulping and manufacturing
processes are expected to conform to the environmental regulations of the
country of origin.

A catalogue record for this book is available from the British Library.

A catalog record for this book is available from the Library of Congress.

10 9 8 7 6 5 4 3 2 1
18 17 16 15 14 13 12 11 10 09

Printed and bound in Great Britain by
CPI Antony Rowe, Chippenham and Eastbourne

CONTENTS

PREFACE

MOST OF US HEAR MUSIC ON A DAILY BASIS, willingly or otherwise, in public spaces or in private. Some of the music we hear is bland, some enjoyable and some exasperating. Yet once in a while, or more often if we are fortunate, we hear music that inspires awe, transfixes us, even stops us in our tracks. Such music, whatever its genre, may be called "sublime" or awe-inspiring. Listeners have recounted being overwhelmed or overpowered by music, being reduced to tears, and experiencing chills or shivers and other bodily sensations. These kinds of experience are the subject of this book.

This book brings together two different intellectual traditions: the philosophical history of the aesthetic sublime and modern empirical research into the phenomenon of strong emotional responses to music. I first became interested in the possibility of investigating strong emotional responses to music at a small conference on the philosophy of music held in south London. There I heard the philosopher Jerrold Levinson read a paper on "chills" caused by music that drew on research by the psychobiologist Jaak Panksepp. Panksepp's research suggested one possible way in which to investigate the types of responses to art and nature that philosophers and critics have since ancient times designated as "sublime." Levinson's paper struck me as exactly the sort of thing philosophers ought to do - to bring together in conversation, if only on paper, people working on the same problem from different angles. The value of such a conversation will be apparent, I hope, in this book. We can learn a lot when specialists in a number of disciplines, including experimental psychology, neuroscience, ethology and the social sciences, are brought together.

Although I started with questions about the power of certain musical works to inspire strong and even disturbing emotional responses, I soon came to see that in order to begin to answer these questions I had to take a step back and think about even broader issues. I found that, ultimately, the question of why some music tends to arouse powerful experiences in some listeners cannot be separated from a more basic question: Why does any music matter at all to anyone? Music's attraction and power over us, I came to believe, stems from its elemental social character. I see musical experience as intrinsically and fundamentally social, rather than personal or individual. Music's social character is evident in the role it plays in every culture, past and present, in creating and reinforcing social bonds, whether these are the bonds between caregivers and infants, adult partners, or among members of social groups and sub-groups. Any so-called "private" experiences of music are derivative, secondary and carry a social meaning. Even listening to music on headphones alone in a room is a social experience through and through. This perspective on music, long supported by anthropologists, is corroborated by recent research in the neurosciences. Attention to the neurobiological foundations of attachment helps us to see how music affects the body, brain and mind in ways which connect listeners in groups and take solitary listeners out of themselves, however briefly. Later in the book I explore the nature of intimacy - a defining feature of some especially significant social relationships - and the role of intimacy in art appreciation in order to see what implications can be drawn for strong emotional experiences of music.

What I have said about the social character of musical experience might strike some as unremarkable. Indeed, I hope it does. However, there is a widespread, but not uncontested, conviction among philosophers of music that the correct philosophical approach to music is to bracket, or set aside, "extra-musical" factors. These might include the lyrics of songs, associations prompted by particular musical works, or the social and material context of listening. It is thought that setting aside these factors allows us to concentrate on the "music itself" - and that this and only this should be the focus of philosophical inquiry. This kind of approach may be a good starting point for certain kinds of philosophical question, but I do not think that it is the best way to understand listeners' experiences. There is no such thing as "music itself" that can be experienced without reference to a context or shared social understandings. If we are to understand listeners' experiences, we must examine all features relevant to those experiences, and we must not decide before proceeding which features can be set aside. Any number of different aspects of the listening experience, apart from the music itself, may contribute to listeners' responses to that music. Yet I do not see such "dense" responses as any less interesting or worthy of investigation for all that. It would be a mistake to conclude that because extra-musical factors contributed to a listener's experience, the music played a merely insignificant role.

* * *

In researching this book I had an opportunity to get better acquainted with the fascinating research on music and the emotions. Music and the emotions have been linked since ancient times, indeed since some of the earliest discussions of emotion in the western tradition. The precise nature of emotion remains very controversial. "Emotion" is both a term of everyday discourse and a technical concept in psychology. This presents a dilemma: the everyday or common-sense understanding of emotion is too vague and amorphous to guide empirical research. Yet to insist on a definition that satisfies all empirical researchers raises a different set of problems. Which definition of emotion should we adopt? Such a strategy also risks taking us unacceptably far from the common-sense understanding of emotion that informs listeners' conceptions of their own experiences. I have tried to steer a course between the sloppiness of everyday usage and the very precise conceptions of emotion employed by some scientists. Sometimes I have used the word "emotions" where a more careful writer would have used the clumsier but more accurate term "affective states."

Researchers whose work is guided by a narrow conception of emotion often take fear to be a paradigmatic emotion. Fear (as opposed to anxiety, wary suspicion, disquiet, trepidation and other related but less intense mental states) has an unambiguous cause or object. (*There is a bear ransacking my campsite!*) A person experiencing fear believes that this object presents a danger. (*If the bear sees me, it will attack!*) Fear guides and energizes behaviour through physiological changes - in this case the adrenaline-fuelled fight-or-flight response. (*I must get out of here right away!*) And it does so in important life situations with serious biological consequences. (*If the bear attacks me, I'm dead!*) The experience of fear and its physical manifestations are thought to be culturally universal. Faced with a similarly frightening stimulus we would expect any other cognitively normal human being to react in a similar way. There is probably a small number of fundamental emotions which are evolutionarily formed and have existed throughout human history and in every culture. These are thought to include fear, anger, disgust, joy and sadness, although researchers disagree both about the number of fundamental emotions and about the exact composition of the list. Of course, the variety of human affective expression is not limited to the fundamental emotions. The range of emotions experienced by any one person and the way that these are expressed are influenced by education and upbringing, so that one's emotional responses are more or less consistent with the norms and expectations of one's culture.

We can distinguish emotions from feelings and moods. "Feelings" or "affects" are the subjective experiential aspect of mental states - that is, how an emotional state feels to the person experiencing it. Some affects are linked closely to the body and are not best thought of as emotions at all - for example, the feelings of hunger and thirst. While most emotions (and all of the fundamental emotions) have physiological aspects, it should be remembered that physiological effects are not, by themselves, sufficient for emotions. Moods are different from emotions in a number of crucial ways. For one thing, moods do not have precise objects, as emotions do. They are less intense than emotions, but at the same time they are pervasive and can colour a person's entire mental outlook. Compare the fear aroused by the sight of a bear ransacking a campsite to a vague sense of dread. Imagine, for example, the dread workers might feel when they come to realize that the industry that employs them may not continue to be economically viable. The mood of anxiety or dread in this case is of much lower intensity than full-blown fear, but it lasts much longer. The workers' dread is likely to be based on a number of factors and to have no single specific cause. It does not prompt a dramatic and physiologically costly fight-or-flight response. The onset of dread was probably gradual rather than sudden. It crept up on the workers, and although the mood may have crystallized at an identifiable instant, there may have been no distinct moment when it intruded into their consciousness. If we keep to a narrow conception of emotion, then it is moods, not emotions, that dominate daily existence.

In thinking about the connections between music and the emotions we need to keep separate two issues: music's capacity to *express* emotion and its power to *induce* or *arouse* emotion. It seems uncontroversial that music can express various emotions - joy, sadness, fear and possibly others. Listeners have little trouble judging the emotional expression of music from their own cultures. Indeed, the emotional expression of music is usually transparently immediate to listeners. We can usually tell readily whether a melody is happy, sad or anxious. This is confirmed both by everyday experience and by psychological research. Even young children are competent judges of emotional expression in their culture's music. However *how*, exactly, music expresses emotion is a tricky issue and has inspired a number of theories. I discuss this question in more detail in chapter 1.

Music's power to arouse emotion is an equally thorny issue. To start with, your view will depend on how generous or restricted a notion of "emotion" you are willing to accept. There are a number of ways in which music might have an effect on listeners' mental states, whether to induce emotions or influence moods. The first is through stimulating physiological changes, including changes in the brain. But as was mentioned earlier, physiological changes are not by themselves sufficient for emotions; so additional factors must be involved. Second, many musical works are associated in the minds of listeners with significant non-musical objects, events or ideas. The memories and associations connected with music can arouse emotions when that music is heard. Such associations may be personal; for example, the memories aroused by hearing a song played at your wedding, or by hearing any music that was important during adolescence or at another significant time of life. Such extra-musical associations may also be shared, as in the case of folk songs, national anthems and any other music that is important to a specific group. Emotions may also be aroused cognitively through a work's structure. Music, as it unfolds in time, creates expectations in the minds of attentive listeners. Composers and performers, in their different ways, manage these expectations, fulfilling, delaying or frustrating them as the case may be. Such "manipulation" of our musical expectations can arouse emotion. Finally, music might arouse emotions that reflect its aesthetic qualities, as distinct from any associations it carries or the physiological changes it induces. We might be irritated by a mediocre work, appalled by a performer's liberties with a beloved standard, awed by an accomplished performance of a very difficult work, or moved by the beauty of an instrument's tone or of a particularly lovely passage. Philosophers have often called such emotions "aesthetic" or specifically "musical" and distinguished them from the emotions of our "everyday" lives.

Many listeners, past and present, report that music stirs their emotions or influences their moods. I would not want to reject their reports, but I am equally reluctant to discount the claims of music lovers who insist that music does *not* regularly arouse their emotions. Some interesting empirical research has been done on these questions by Vladimir Konečni and two of his graduate students at the University of California, San Diego. Participants were asked to spend three minutes remembering a particularly happy or sad event from their past. They were then asked to rate how happy or sad they felt during the event, and how happy or sad they feel recalling the event for the purpose of the experiment. Next, the participants who had been asked to recall a happy event listened to a three-minute excerpt of happy music, and those who had been asked to recall a sad event listened to an excerpt of sad music. Finally, participants were asked to rate how happy or sad the music made them feel. Participants gave the highest ratings - they felt happiest and saddest - during the happy or sad event from their past. They felt less intensely emotional remembering the happy or sad event, and still less emotional after listening to music. It seems, then, that when most listeners take a broader perspective, the emotional effects of music generally pale in comparison to those of "real-life" events.

What can we learn about music and emotion from this research? Listeners' claims to be emotionally aroused by music must be analysed carefully. It is reasonable to ask what factors, in addition to "music itself," might be involved. And if listeners continue to talk about music and their experiences of it in emotional terms, despite what seems like evidence that music does not readily arouse emotion, it is also reasonable to ask why this should be so.

* * *

The first chapter, "The Tears of Odysseus," goes over some ancient and still pertinent ideas about music: ideas about music's capacity to provoke strong emotions, its influence on the soul and its power even over evil spirits. Indeed, music's purported power and its ability to act directly on the soul have made it an object of concern for moralists from ancient Greece to the present day. Religious thinkers throughout history have been ambivalent about music, seeing it sometimes as a potential conduit to the divine and at other times as sensual indulgence. This is true of both the Judeo-Christian and the Islamic traditions. We also see a connection between music and the divine in the close association, in many parts of the world, between music and trance states. Finally, both kinds of belief about music - its capacity to act directly on the soul and its connection with the divine - come together in the characterization of music as sublime, and I explore the different ways in which music might be said to be sublime. From then on, the focus of the book is listeners' experiences of the sublime.

Chapter 2, "History: Music Gives Voice to the Ineffable," covers the history of the concept of the sublime. We track its progression from ancient times through its philosophical heyday in the eighteenth century up to its peak of importance for music in the late nineteenth century. We touch on the thought of Longinus, Edmund Burke, Immanuel Kant and others. Music was not generally considered to be sublime until the late eighteenth century. By then, music had gone from being the servant of texts to inhabiting its own world, beyond mere words. Considerable cultural and philosophical change had to occur before it became even plausible that music could be considered sublime. We shall see that the most important of these changes have their roots in Kant's philosophical aesthetics. During the same period, listeners went from being seen as more or less passive recipients of a composer's art, to shouldering great burdens of musical sensitivity and comprehension. It became incumbent on them to understand, and composers to communicate.

At the heart of chapter 3, "Tears, Chills, and Broken Bones," are a number of descriptions of strong emotional responses to music. Many of these are first-person accounts, to let listeners speak for themselves and to convey as much as possible what such experiences are like from the inside. Sublime or emotionally strong responses range from momentary chills or thrills to enduring, deeply affecting, even "out-of-body" experiences. Such experiences can feel to the listener to be intensely personal and private, or they might be boisterously social and communal. Sometimes music is seen as dominating the experience; at other times it is one factor among many. Although each of the experiences described is different, there is more commonality among them than might be expected. When experiences differ, they tend to differ in specific respects. At the end of this chapter we look at some of the difficulties inherent in relying on listeners' testimonies and consider whether possible objections can be overcome.

When listeners are asked about the music that has aroused strong emotions in them or struck them as sublime, they mention many different kinds of music: classical or art music, pop and non-western music; symphonic works and solo compositions; and pieces from the baroque era, the romantic period and the twentieth century. Chapter 4, "The Music Itself," examines some of these works and what they have in common. I begin with music thought to bring about trance states, as these are among the most extreme responses to music. Then I take a look at some studies by psychologists on music that arouses chills or shivers and tears. It turns out that a number of structural features can be linked with these responses. Finally, I say something about the expressive and aesthetic qualities of music thought to bring about strong responses. While there are specific musical-structural and sonic features associated with strong emotional responses, we shall see that these in themselves cannot fully explain the phenomenon.

So how, then, might we explain strong emotional responses to music? In chapters 5 and 6, "Explaining Strong Emotional Responses to Music"

(I and II), I begin to answer this question. Chapter 5 clears the ground for my own view, which is laid out in chapter 6. First, we take a look at some of the reductive explanations that have been offered, starting with a reductive explanation of trance states. Many reductive explanations rely on what has been called the "pharmaceutical model" of musical understanding, whereby music stimulates listeners in much the way that a drug would. The glaring problem with this model is that music, of course, is not a drug. We do not merely "react" to music, but hear it with more or less understanding and appreciation, and our understanding and appreciation grow as our knowledge of music improves. Next, we take a look at some of the more plausible explanations that have been offered, including cognitive accounts and expressive-aesthetic accounts. Chapter 5 ends with a shift in the discussion from the question of why some music arouses strong responses in some listeners, to the nature of music more generally. Before we can understand why a particular work might be considered to be sublime, we have to understand why any music at all might be. One of the key things that needs to be taken into consideration, it turns out, is music's fundamentally social nature.

Chapter 6 starts with an investigation of what this amounts to, and how it is that even solitary listening to music is best conceived of as a social phenomenon. From there, we explore the links between music and social bonding among both humans and other animals. In every culture that we know of, adults sing to children and babies and speak to them in a characteristically "musical" manner. Music contributes to attachment between infants and caregivers, and to different kinds of social bonds among adults. A deeper investigation of social bonding leads us to consider the brain mechanisms that underwrite attachment behaviour, and the effects of music on the brain more broadly. This is complemented by a look at some of the important cognitive aspects of absorption in music. What is it about music as an object for the mind that makes it so effective at drawing listeners in and taking them out of themselves? The chapter ends with a discussion of the nature of intimacy - a feature of some especially important social relations - and of what role intimacy might play in art and music appreciation.

The final two chapters - "The Sublime, Revisited" and the concluding chapter "Values" - take us back to more evaluative concerns, including the connections between music and morality. What are the relations among the sublime, beauty, artistic value and emotion in music? We also take a look at profundity, and what might be meant when listeners or critics claim that a particular work is "profound." Can music be profound in the same way that a poem or a scientific discovery might be? Is any one kind of music of greater moral worth than another? Finally, how important are strong emotional experiences of music? How highly should we value the sublime in music? And what might have happened when music of great artistic quality *fails* to move listeners?

Acknowledgements

This book had its origins in a Social Sciences and Humanities Research Council of Canada postdoctoral fellowship. I want first to thank Jerrold Levinson whose work originally inspired me to take up this research project. He has been a source of encouragement and philosophical insight since his initial agreement to supervise my postdoctoral research, through early discussions, and then reading and commenting on several earlier versions of this material. His commitment to mentoring younger scholars sets a very high standard.

I am very grateful to the following people: Joseph Agassi, Evan Cameron, Alf Gabrielsson, Roberta Morris, Saam Trivedi, and two anonymous referees for reading and commenting on an earlier draft in its entirety; Mario Bunge, Louis Groarke, Phil Jenkins, Vladimir Konečni, Ron Moore and William Rottschaefer for reading and commenting on shorter passages; Ted Bond, John Brown, Ted Gracyk, Patricia Greenspan, Vladimir Konečni, Yakov Lerner, Judith Lichtenberg, Justin London, Peter Morgan and Forrest Pierce for discussions of philosophical issues or music (or both); Boris Bohuslawsky, Tracey Nasato, Roberta Morris, Indu Singh, Eva Smith and Ruth Willats for help in editing the final version of the manuscript; Daniel Bunyard, formerly of Palgrave Macmillan, for his early support of the project and for suggesting some important structural changes, and to Priyanka Pathak who stepped in at Palgrave Macmillan after Daniel's departure and suggested numerous improvements. I would also like to mention my gratitude to Evan Cameron, Robert Hanna, Joseph Gonda, my doctoral supervisory committee at York University in Toronto, Canada, for their unstinting encouragement and support since I entered the profession, and for their influence on my philosophical development.

Finally, I want to acknowledge the contribution of my immediate family: my husband, Ian Jarvie, who has now patiently read and commented on several versions of this project and suggested numerous improvements, sometimes setting aside his own work; and my daughter Madeleine, who always helps me keep things in perspective. This book is dedicated to them.

1

THE TEARS OF ODYSSEUS

ODYSSEUS AND THE BARD

HOMER TELLS US THAT ODYSSEUS spent seven years on the island of Ogygia pining for his home, a prisoner of the beautiful nymph Calypso. Through the intervention of the goddess Athena he is finally allowed to leave. At sea he encounters a fierce storm and the boat which he has built to make his escape is wrecked. Exhausted and naked, Odysseus swims to the shore of the land of the Phaeacians, which is ruled by the good King Alcinous. Alcinous grants Odysseus protection and hospitality, even staging a banquet in his honour. The famous bard Demodocus is present, and when everyone has had their fill of food and drink, Demodocus sings. Odysseus listens to his song and weeps.

Why does Odysseus weep? Perhaps because the subject of the bard's song has strong personal associations for him. Demodocus sings of the quarrel between Odysseus and Achilles, and of King Agamemnon's secret delight at their falling out. Are Odysseus' tears, then, a response solely to the words of the song? After all, no one else present at the banquet weeps; indeed, the other guests urge Demodocus to continue. Or perhaps Odysseus weeps simply because he is physically and psychologically exhausted by his long struggle to return home. There is another possibility: Homer, himself a bard, here makes a reflexive comment on the power of his art. Odysseus weeps not for purely personal reasons, but in response to artistic creation - words and music combined in song, performed with skill and sensitivity.

Odysseus' crying ceases when Demodocus stops singing, and his tears flow once more when the song recommences. Ashamed of his tears, he covers his face with his cloak. His response to the song is powerful. Forceful sobs and heavy sighs indicate a loss of control, which Odysseus can neither temper nor forestall, but can only attempt to conceal. Alcinous, seated next to Odysseus, notices his guest's discomfort. He proposes that Demodocus stop singing and suggests that the group leave the banqueting hall and play sports instead.

The ancient Greeks held strong views about music's power over the emotions, and about the connections among music, ethical character and action. When Agamemnon set out for the Trojan War he commanded a bard to keep guard over his young wife, Clytemnestra. The bard's music was supposed to reinforce Clytemnestra's naturally good disposition and ensure her faithfulness to her husband. It is only when Agamemnon's rival Aegisthus banishes the bard to a desert island that Clytemnestra betrays her husband's trust.

The various musical modes were thought to have quite predictable and specific emotional effects upon listeners. Several versions of the following story are told and retold throughout antiquity. One night a group of youths had been out drinking. One of them, a young man from Taormina, became frenzied on hearing music in the Phrygian mode. Passing his rival's home and learning that he was entertaining a prostitute, the young man became enraged and threatened to set fire to his rival's house. His friends tried to dissuade him but it did no good. The philosopher Pythagoras, out observing the motion of the stars, came upon the scene and directed the musicians to play instead a melody in the Dorian mode. The young man's mood changed from frenzied anger to perfect calm; the change in musical mode restored his self-mastery.

In another version of the story, recounted by Cicero, a group of drunken youths were aroused by the sound of the tibiae, an ancient wind instrument that is the ancestor of the modern oboe. They were about to break into the house of a virtuous woman when Pythagoras urged the musician to play a melody in a different mode. It is said that the slowness and gravity of the music calmed the youths' "wanton fury." In other versions of the story it is not Pythagoras, but the renowned music theorist Damon who commands the musicians and restores calm.

Boethius, the neo-Pythagorean philosopher and poet, recounts both versions of the story in his *Fundamentals of Music*, written at the beginning of the sixth century. This work was rediscovered in the Renaissance and had a great influence on later thinking about music. Boethius expected his readers to be familiar with the story, and he treats the effects of music on the body and mind as entirely commonplace.

MUSIC AND THE SOUL

The Hebrew Bible (I Samuel 16:14-23) relates that when King Saul was tormented by an evil spirit, his attendants proposed that they search for someone who could play the harp. One of the servants suggested David, who was duly summoned. Whenever the spirit afflicted Saul, David would play the harp. David's music had the desired effect: Saul's suffering was lifted and he found relief.

Modern readers are likely to psychologize this incident. Saul's "evil spirit" reflects a quaint or pre-scientific understanding of mental illness, and David is an early music therapist. Listening to the harp, Saul momentarily escapes his cares and worries. Or David's music might be seen as an expression of his compassion for the older man, a potent reminder of how music can serve to bring people together. These interpretations share an understanding of music's power as benign or beneficial. But consider the incident once more. What is happening, on the surface? The implication is that music has causal powers greater than those of an evil spirit. Moreover, it is the only power that seems great enough to banish the spirit.

There is an ancient tradition according to which music has the ability to provoke profound, even disturbing reactions - tears, trembling, collapse. Music would seem to be able to overwhelm reason and act directly on the soul. In the description of hearing offered in Plato's *Timaeus*, sound is a percussion of air that is transmitted to the soul by way of the ears and the brain. The motion caused by the percussion begins in the head and ends in the liver. According to the ancients, the liver was the seat of vitality and of the emotions. Hence sound directly affects physical and mental well-being, presumably for good or ill.

Music's purported power to act directly on the soul has long made it a source of concern for moralists and religious thinkers. According to Plato, Socrates thought the effects of music on emotion and character to be serious enough that he would have banned certain musical modes from his ideal city. In the *Laws* we are told that no one will be allowed to sing a song, no matter how sweet, if it has not been first approved by the rulers. Aristotle, Plato's student, ends his *Politics* with a discussion of musical education and the role of music-making in the life of a free man.

Ancient Greek views on music influenced later Christian and Islamic thinkers. St. Augustine's writings on music are in many ways exemplary of the Christian tradition. They betray a deep ambivalence towards music as both a source of great beauty and spiritual succour, and a potentially dangerous temptation from God's path. As a young man before his conversion Augustine loved the arts and especially the music of the theatre. After his conversion to Christianity he came to see his younger self as unwillingly "bound" to the pleasures of music. Conversion brought him freedom from music's power; he could find repose in it without also "clinging" to it. In his *Confessions*, Augustine movingly describes the effect on himself of music heard in church: "The voices flowed into my ears; and the truth was poured forth into my heart, where the tide of my devotion overflowed, and my tears ran down, and I was happy in all these things." But the music of worship could have a different effect on Augustine. He reproached himself for sometimes attending more to "beguiling" melodies than to the holy words. "Yet when it happens that I am more moved by the singing than by what is sung," he writes, "I confess myself to have sinned wickedly, and then I would rather not have heard the singing." At such moments, Augustine found himself sympathetic to those who would banish singing from the church altogether. Yet at the same time he was inclined to think that music was an appropriate part of worship, "so that by the delights of the ear the weaker minds may be stimulated to a devotional mood."

Medieval Islamic thinkers were similarly ambivalent about music. The rich and wide-ranging literature on the legal and theological admissibility of music contains views ranging from full acceptance to complete negation. There is nothing in the Koran specifically about music, and thinkers drawing on the Hadith (the tradition of anecdotes about Mohammed's life and pronouncements) sometimes interpret the same story so as to justify very different conclusions. The arguments offered for and against music would have been familiar to the Christian Church Fathers, as well as to earlier Greek thinkers. On the one hand, music offers a sensual indulgence that can tempt the mind away from God. On the other hand, the beauty of music can be used to emphasize holy words, thereby bringing listeners closer to God. The great philosopher and theologian al'Ghazzali, after analysing the huge number of contrasting arguments, came to the conclusion that music was permissible for seven purposes but forbidden for five. Appropriate uses of music include to encourage pilgrimage, to incite to battle and inspire courage, to evoke sorrow, joy, love and longing (in circumstances in which these emotions are appropriate) and to evoke love of God. Music was forbidden, however, if listened to for its own sake.

Throughout the Islamic tradition writers stressed music's overwhelming and irresistible power over listeners. Music was seen as capable of producing such great sensual pleasure or profound excitement that listeners might lose control of their reason and succumb to passions. The word *tarab* referred to a range of possible emotional responses to music - everything from delicate pleasure to strong excitement and even ecstasy. Although this term was originally applied to the emotions stirred by the fine recitation of a beautiful poem, it later became identified with music and its derivates. A musician is a *mutrib* and musical instruments *'alat al-tarab*.

MUSIC AND THE DIVINE

The discomfort of both Christian and Muslim thinkers reminds us of the association, seemingly cross-cultural and transhistorical, of music with the divine. In all cultures that we know of, music has some connection with ritual, religion and the supernatural. In St Augustine's time theatre performances and music were strongly associated with pagan worship and rites, and this perhaps helps account for his post-conversion suspicion of music. The Hebrew Bible contains numerous mentions of music as a part of both pagan and Jewish ritual life and worship, and music was also an important component of ancient Greek religious practices. It would seem that little has changed. Although different Christian confessions may disagree about which music is appropriate for worship and over the admissibility of musical instruments in church, even the most austere allow unaccompanied singing.

Music continues to play an important role in ritual, whether religious or secular. Major public civil and military ceremonies are accompanied by music. In private life, no wedding celebration, funeral or memorial service is complete without music. For some couples, the choice of the song for their first dance together as a married couple is as important a decision as the content of their vows. Music is heard at initiation ceremonies such as baptisms, bar and bat mitzvahs, school graduations and commencements. (Those who are, like me, a former member of a school band or orchestra may remember performing "Pomp and Circumstance" over and over until the last graduates retrieved their diplomas.) Those who have the *sang-froid* to plan their own memorial services often specify which music should be played. Even athletic events have ritualistic aspects accompanied by music: performance of national anthems, musical acts at halftime, musical riffs to rev up the crowd and communal singing in the stands.

The use of music in ritual surely derives from its perceived connections with the divine or the spiritual realm. Music has long been seen as a means of invoking the gods. To give only one example, in II Kings, 3, the prophet Elisha summons a harpist when called upon by King Joram to reveal the will of the Lord. The enduring connection between music and the divine is seen in the title of a recent book, *I'll Take You There: Pop Music and the Urge for Transcendence*. Even a song as unabashedly carnal as Marvin Gaye's "Let's Get it On" is argued to be ultimately not about sex, but about true connections with the beloved, and possibly even with God. Not everyone will find such a take on the song plausible; spiritual and transcendental elements are taken to be more readily found in "classical" and explicitly religious music than in popular songs. Yet it can hardly be denied that many composers and musicians working in a variety of musical idioms, both historically and today, see their musical activity in religious or spiritual terms.

In the western tradition the attitude to music as a conduit to the spiritual realm goes hand-in-hand with the perception of the composer as creative genius and the virtuoso performer as divinely (or devilishly) inspired. The violinist Nicolo Pagininni and legendary blues guitarist Robert Johnson are only two instrumentalists rumoured to owe their amazing technique to a pact with the devil. While these attitudes had their highest expression in nineteenth-century Romanticism, we are hardly free of them today. The sociological commonplace of the arena or concert hall as church and the concert as ritual is almost too familiar to merit a mention.

A different kind of connection between music and the spiritual realm is to be found in the close association in many parts of the world between music and certain altered states of consciousness. Whether called trance states, ecstasy or raptures, such states are temporary, more or less prolonged, and usually brought about by sensory over-stimulation. They are most often evoked as part of religious rituals and people who have experienced such states typically have no memory of them. There is no generally accepted terminology distinguishing the different altered states of consciousness, and different writers with various purposes may use different terms. To make matters more com-plicated, translations of the relevant terms from foreign languages into English are also inconsistent. For the sake of simplicity, I will refer to all such states of consciousness involving music as "trance states." Trance states invariably occur in social contexts and are to be distinguished from solitary mystical experiences. Solitary mystical experiences are typically evoked by silence, immobility and sensory deprivation. They may be accompanied by hallucinations and are typically recalled by the mystic. Indeed, there is a rich autobiographical literature by mystics, but very few autobiographical accounts of trance states.

The universality of trance states in very different cultural and reli-gious traditions indicates that it corresponds to a "psychophysiological disposition" innate in human nature. That is, given the right prep-aration and conditions, nearly anyone will experience a trance state. The frenzy brought about in the youth from Taormina in response to music in the Phrygian mode sounds very much like a trance state. Phrygia was the homeland of Dionysius, and religious practices in his cult included inducing trance states through music and dance. The story of the afflicted youth likely strikes us as little more than an historical curiosity, but beliefs about the power of music to give access to the spiritual realm via altered states of consciousness have been extremely robust. As late as the seventeenth century they were an important part of the debate in England over the admissibility of musical instruments and polyphonic singing in church. Defenders of musical instruments argued that their playing contributed directly to the union of the worshipper with God. The idea that music could bring about ecstasy or rapture and separate the soul from the body appears repeatedly in English poetry and prose of the period. For some, especially later writers, the idea is evoked as no more than a literary device; yet in others it is a provocative theory to be given serious consideration, if not strict acceptance. Shakespeare's Benedick is showing real interest in a contemporary debate when he asks:

> Now, divine air! Now is his soul ravished!
> Is it not strange that sheeps' guts should hale
> Souls out of men's bodies?
>
> (*Much Ado About Nothing* II. iii. 60-2)

Just as Muslim writers debating the admissibility of music came to different conclusions when they interpreted stories in the Hadith, so too did seventeenth-century English writers defend different interpretations of the story of Saul and David. Participants on both sides of the debate understood the story more or less literally. Those who argued for the acceptance of musical instruments pointed to the story as evidence of music's power over spirits, including souls, as it was the music of the harp that banished the evil spirit. After all, Saul's servants would not have advised him to seek out a harpist had they not known about the power of music over the soul. Those who believed that musical instruments had no place in church argued that music's power was over the ear (and, by extension, the sensual body) and that music could not by itself induce spiritual thoughts. The power of David's music must have been in the words of his song rather than the instrumental accompaniment. (This, despite the fact that there is no suggestion in the text that David sang for Saul.) Opponents of music argued that it was God, not David, who drove out the evil spirit. Another possibility was that the evil spirit took advantage of Saul's melancholy to torment him; when David's music cheered and refreshed Saul the evil spirit simply left him alone.

MUSIC AND THE SUBLIME

These beliefs about music - that it can be a direct and powerful influence on human emotions and its association with the divine - are complementary. Indeed, they come together in the characterization of music as sublime, and in the attitudes and experiences which support this characterization.

The word "sublime" has two related senses. First, it denotes a human emotion - a feeling of overwhelming awe aroused by the contemplation of a particularly magnificent, large or powerful object or event. Second, "sublime" describes those objects and events (or some set of their attributes) which are thought to arouse the feeling of the sublime. Such objects and events might be natural (mountains, thunderstorms, grand vistas, the raging sea) or made by humans (imposing buildings, overgrown ruins, great works of art). Some writers have described the feeling of the sublime as one of pleasure mingled with pain, or at least discomfort. Historically, sublime objects and experiences have been thought capable of subverting human rationality. Their ability to confound mental powers or get under the skin was seen as their most significant feature. The sublime has often been linked with religion and with feelings of insignificance before God. Sublime objects and the feelings they arouse have been thought to bring human beings closer to the Divine.

The sublime was a leading topic of eighteenth-century aesthetics although its greatest influence on musical discourse would have to wait a little longer. Currently, it is enjoying a period of renewed philosophical interest and respectability. One indication of this is that the entry on "the sublime" in Routledge's most recent *Encyclopedia of Philosophy* is several pages long. The 1967 *Encyclopedia* did not even include a separate entry on the sublime. Music and the sublime can come together in a number of ways; certain music might itself be sublime, or it might inspire feelings of the sublime in listeners. Exploring the sublimity of music takes us to the very heart of issues in the philosophy of music: What is music, exactly? What sort of feelings can it arouse? Can it represent non-musical phenomena? Are there limits to what musicians and composers can convey through music? What is the relationship between music as heard and music as notated? What are the different contributions of performers and composers to what we hear? How has the development of recording technology affected our enjoyment and understanding of music? What accounts for music's presence, throughout history and in our own time, in every known culture?

Each of these questions deserves and would surely reward serious consideration. Rather than offer a precise definition, I propose to understand "music" in a fairly wide sense and take the term as neutral or descriptive rather than as evaluative. There are considerable practical difficulties involved in trying to arrive at a clear-cut definition of music. Are the birds that sing at dawn making music? Would the answer be different if someone were to record the birds, package the results with tasteful cover art and sell it at the local CD shop? In the developed West, music is usually taken to be a product of human agency, but this is not so across the globe. Different cultures can have very different ideas about what constitutes music. Most preliterate peoples seem to conceive of the words and melody of a song as inseparable, and in some cultures music has an indispensable gestural component. For example, traditional Ghanian "music" includes drumming, dancing and singing, which are together considered one thing. In the developed West, avant-garde composers have repeatedly challenged and expanded the boundaries of what critics and audiences consider music, and there is every likelihood that they will continue to do so.

While any sound can be listened to *as if* it were music; it does not follow that any and every sound *actually is* music. The most adequate philosophical definition of music that I have come across is that of Jerrold Levinson. It is intended to cover pretty much everything traditionally understood to be music, as well as avant-garde music and

the various phenomena studied by ethnomusicologis
inition has three key components. First, music is h
sound. He thus excludes birdsong and whale "music."
ing issues hinge on whether or not we take the soun
non-human animals to be music, and I think that this
need to keep an open mind about. (I will come back to the question in
a later chapter.) Second, in music sound is organized for the purpose
of enriching or intensifying experience through active engagement.
This is the "central core" of the music-making intention; those who
make music mean for others to pay attention to it. "Engagement" here
might include singing or playing along, dancing or listening. Finally,
the organized sounds are to be regarded primarily, or in significant
measure, as sounds. This condition is meant to exclude, for example,
the recitation of poetry or the delivery of a sermon. In these cases,
listeners attend to meaning of organized sounds; that is, listeners are
meant to attend to the meaning of the words, rather than primarily to
the sound qualities of the words as they are spoken.

In formulating his definition of music in this way, Levinson avoids
an important philosophical pitfall. To provide defining characteristics for music - properties which are shared by all music and only
by music - risks treating music as a natural kind. That is, treating it
as a class delimited by natural law rather than by social convention.
Fortunately, a working or "rough-and-ready" understanding of music
is adequate. Surely most people have some idea (however vague)
of what music is, and the fact that most would likely not survive a
Socratic inquisition on the nature of music with their beliefs intact
should not be troubling.

More pressing for an investigation of music and the sublime is the
question of to what extent (if at all) music can be said to *represent*
non-musical (or even non-auditory) objects and events. The ancient
Greeks believed that all art, including music, was mimetic or imita-
tive. In Book X of Plato's *Republic* Socrates derisively compares the
artist to a copyist who might just as well "imitate" nature by walking
around holding up a mirror. Music was also thought to be mimetic
and to represent states of the soul - one source of its troubling power
over human beings. If music is indeed capable of representation, then

ᵗnnection between music and the sublime might be that some ᵗsic (entire works or sections of them) *represents* objects and events already described as sublime in other contexts. If it is plausible that music can represent non-auditory properties, objects and events, then there is potentially no limit to the things music might be said to represent. A musical representation of the sublime might be a representation of mountains, waterfalls, the raging sea, the vastness of the universe, etc.

But is it plausible to think that music can represent such things? There is no doubt that composers have attempted to convey non-auditory properties and objects through music, but this does not settle the issue. As with any philosophical question, much hangs on the precise understanding of key terms. If by "to represent" is meant something like "to make a likeness of" or "to depict," then the scope of musical representation will be limited to the representation of sounds: train whistles, birdsong, babbling brooks perhaps. However, there is no reason to accept such a circumscribed understanding of representation. Not all "representations" look like the things they are supposed to represent. We understand the characters "Uncle Sam" and "John Bull" respectively to represent the United States and England in political cartoons, despite the fact that a person wearing archaic clothing and a top hat does not resemble a country. We understand the representation because at one point the association was made, then became widely accepted and is now a convention. In learning how to interpret political cartoons we learned this and other conventions. Musical representations can also be secured through stipulation and convention. For example, a fanfare on horns has come to represent the hunt. Wagnerian leitmotifs and the use of descriptive titles are forms of stipulation used to secure musical representation. Another possible form of musical representation is through an underlying structural similarity between properties of music and properties of the object to be represented. For example, the ascent of a melodic line might represent a physical ascent; a lurching rhythm might represent a lurching gait; a slow, ponderous and grave melody might represent the movements of a sad person.

Whether or not a particular attempt at musical representation is successful will have to be decided on a case-by-case basis. There are several examples of musical attempts to represent sublime objects. These include Mendelssohn's *Hebrides Overture*; Richard Strauss's *Alpensymphonie* (a tone poem describing a day in the mountains - instrumentation includes wind and thunder machines); the fourth movement of Beethoven's *Pastoral Symphony*, part of which is meant to represent a thunderstorm; Debussy's *La Mer* (and works by other composers which represent the sea); Stravinsky's *The Rite of Spring* (ballet music based on a libretto about a pagan ritual in which a chosen sacrificial victim dances herself to death); and the music of the "Confutatis" section of Mozart's *Requiem*, evoking the horrors of Hell.

The question of how and what music can *express* is no less conceptually fraught than the question of how and what it might represent. Some philosophers have argued that music cannot express anything, as it is not a sentient being and only sentient beings are capable of expression. Hence any talk of musical "expression" must be fundamentally confused or merely metaphorical. This is not a position that I can support; I see nothing amiss with ordinary, unphilosophical talk of music's being sad, happy, anxious, etc. While the verb "to express" may have been originally restricted to sentient beings, it does not follow that the only proper use of the term remains in reference to sentient beings. But if we agree that music can express, then we owe an explanation of just what this means and how it is achieved.

One account - the arousal theory - holds that music expresses an emotion when it arouses similar or related emotions in listeners. Derek Matravers has offered the most fully worked-out version of the arousal theory. Matravers qualifies the view in a number of important ways that make it more plausible. He stresses that he has in mind the arousal of feeling in "qualified" listeners - those who have the relevant musical and cultural background to understand the music in question and who are listening under normal conditions. When such listeners hear, say, sad music, their response is the arousal of pity - the same feeling that would be appropriate in response to the expression of sadness by a human being. Although the view that music expresses the emotions or feelings it arouses may have some intuitive appeal, it will not suffice as an account of expression in music. For one thing it is not clear that music arouses emotion in all qualified and attentive listeners. When emotion is felt by listeners, this does not necessarily correspond to the emotions heard in the music. Listeners might be irritated or bored by sad music, or inexplicably saddened by a cheerful tune. Another difficulty for the arousal theory is that not everything that arouses one's feelings is thereby expressive. I am frightened of the bear that is ransacking my campsite, but it does not follow that the bear is expressive of fear or "scariness." In his most recent thoughts on the subject, Matravers admits that his views have not been widely adopted.

A more plausible account of musical expression is cognitivism, and it is most strongly associated with the philosopher Peter Kivy. According to the cognitive theory of musical expression, we recognize emotion in music as a perceptual property of the music. Kivy appeals to a photograph of a St Bernard dog to help explain what this amounts to. The dog's face is expressive of sadness; this is not to say that she actually is sad or that looking at her will arouse sadness in us. Rather, her drooping face and liquid eyes seem appropriate to the expression of sadness; her expression looks like one that might be on the face of a sad person. Similarly, according to Kivy, music is expressive in virtue of its resemblance to expressive human utterance and behaviour. For example, certain vocal and bodily patterns are typical of sad people - they tend to speak slowly, in low tones, and move as though under strain. Music expressive of sadness will resemble these features - it will likely be slow and in a low register.

"Sublime" traditionally designates a quality of feeling as well as a property of objects. If music can indeed express emotion, then there is no reason in principle why composers could not attempt to express the feeling of the sublime in their music. If successful, such music would express the feeling that a person has when confronted with an awe-inspiring object. Whether or not the composer succeeded would have to be decided on a case-by-case basis. It is also possible that music could express the sublime without this having been the composer's specific intention. Listeners might find certain musical passages expressive of the sublime whether or not the composer meant for them to be heard in this way, or even himself had a concept of the sublime. This would be the case for almost all music composed prior to the eighteenth century which today's listeners find expressive of the sublime.

Music and the sublime have an *adverbial* connection when a work or performance is said to be "sublimely," say, beautiful or sad. A quick search of the Internet came up with many such examples, including descriptions of music as "sublimely lovely," "sublimely perfect," "sublimely rueful," "sublimely deep," "sublimely intelligent," "sublimely tranquil," "sublimely disturbing," "sublimely funky" and "sublimely poised between ungainliness and elegance." It might be the case that "sublimely" is used in these and other instances simply as an intensifier (in place of "extremely," for example). On the other hand, the speaker may be trying to name a particular quality of the music, over and above its beauty or sadness. Both conclusions are possible, and we could not be sure which was meant without consulting the writer.

A further possibility is that the locus of sublimity is musical *performances* rather than works, or in addition to works. If the goal of a performance is to be faithful to the work, is the best performance of a banal work one that allows listeners to recognize its banality? Those interested in the philosophical aspects of musical performance disagree as to whether performers' primary obligations are to audiences or to composers. Sometimes a (seemingly) simple work can be performed with such skill and sensitivity that it will strike listeners as sublime. The same work performed by a different (perhaps less skilled or sensitive) performer would not arouse such feelings. Has a very fine performance allowed listeners to recognize a seemingly unremarkable work as sublime? Or has the performer brought to the work something not actually "there" to begin with? Although it seems paradoxical, we might also allow for the possibility that a particular performance could be sublime, even if the work performed is not. This might happen when we are impressed by a dazzling technical display that occurs in the performance of a work that is without much musical interest. We might also say that a work is sublime only "in" a particular performance. No doubt readers will have their favourite performances to refer to here. The examples which come most readily to my mind are from jazz: John Coltrane's variations on Rodgers and Hammerstein's "My Favorite Things" and Miles Davis's version of the Disney favourite "Someday My Prince Will Come."

One of the most common associations of music with sublimity occurs in *evaluative* or *critical* usage, where it is a term of great praise and applied to artists and composers as different as Mozart and the avant-garde pop group Art of Noise. Beethoven's music is routinely praised as sublime. The philosopher Theodore Gracyk claims of the Sex Pistols' "Bodies": "These three minutes of rock are truly sublime." The music writer Jan Swafford refers to the "sublime final aria" of Bach's *St. Matthew Passion* ("Come my heart and make thee clean that my Jesus I may bury.") To say that a work or performance is sublime is to say (at least) that it is very good or has a high artistic value. But is anything else meant? Usage is not systematic enough to answer this definitively. Sometimes it would seem that a writer is indicating a certain quality or power in the music beyond its excellence, but we would have to consult the particular author to be sure.

Now, I am not a relativist - someone who believes that all aesthetic judgements are strictly matters of personal taste and that it is impossible to make a judgement that one musical work is better or worse than another. The problem lies, however, in how to cash out the notion of "better" and how one might convince others who disagree that a certain work really is better. Yet, the question of whether a musical work or performance is good or indifferent is a different question from whether it is moving to listeners, and we have to keep this in mind. I will not have much to say about the relative merits of different musical works, styles and traditions. Since I am not a music critic, these questions are really out of my purview.

LISTENERS AND THE SUBLIME

When Odysseus weeps he does so, not in response to the song of any bard, but in response to Demodocus, the bard whom the Muses love above all others. Later it will become evident that there is some overlap (but not total concurrence) between the works and performances critics praise very highly and those that tend to arouse strong feelings in listeners. This kind of *listener's response* will be the main subject of this book. Among the music most of us hear everyday, willingly or otherwise, in public spaces and private, some is tolerable, some merely pleasant and some exasperating. Yet once in a while, or often if we are fortunate, we hear music that inspires awe, transfixes us, even stops us in our tracks.

Listeners have recounted being overwhelmed or overpowered by the music, being reduced to tears, and experiencing chills or shivers and other bodily sensations. Clearly, some music has the ability to get under our defences. Such music, whatever its genre, may be said to arouse an experience of the sublime. Listeners may use the word "sublime" to describe such music and their responses to it, but not necessarily. In the following chapters we shall examine these responses and the music which arouses them. To do this we shall need to draw on seemingly unrelated research in various disciplines, including psychology, neuroscience and anthropology. What is going on when we have a sublime or strong emotional response to music? Are there structural features in musical works that induce these responses? What, if anything, do such responses mean? Can they tell us anything about music or about ourselves? In the course of this investigation we shall need to come to grips with topics as seemingly disparate as strong emotion and "disinterested" aesthetic response; individual personality and the social norms guiding audience behaviour; the importance of tradition and a common culture in mediating listeners' responses; the human body and brain as natural objects of scientific study; the human mind as cultural artefact; aesthetic value and the mystery of beauty.

The term "sublime" is more at home in discussions of nature and literature than in the psychology of listening, so some readers might wonder about the appropriateness of its use here. Instead of offering a peremptory answer, I hope that the rest of this book will provide such a justification. The term "sublime" both designates the special character of the experiences we shall examine and connects them with a specific cultural and historical milieu. Still, if it is not presumptuous, I will repeat the defence offered by the philosopher Baruch (Benedict) Spinoza to the charge that the characterizations he gave of certain emotions in his *Ethics* were not what was ordinarily understood of those emotions. He countered that it was because he was interested not in the meaning of words, but in the nature of things.

That said, there are other ways in which to approach the sublime. Before continuing I want to say something about two possible strategies that are different from mine. The first is from a philosopher and the second from a psychologist.

The philosopher Julian Young has argued that Martin Heidegger's work on the sublime is the culmination of about two hundred years of philosophical writing on the subject. Previous accounts have been inadequate in different ways. Heidegger's account is superior because he rejects the metaphysical foundations shared by earlier thinkers. According to Young, the feeling of the sublime is Freud's "oceanic" feeling. It is an expansion of the self, "a flowing out of the ego and into the totality of things." Heidegger's account alone is able to capture these subtleties.

I have no quarrel with Young over his interpretation of Heidegger or any other thinker. I have chosen to discuss him because he provides a clear example of philosophical essentialism. The "essence" of a thing is that which makes it what it is. For example, it is "essential" that a square has four sides of equal length, set at right angles. Squares may be any colour or size; but if a shape does not have four equal sides set at right angles, then it is not a square. But what holds true of squares - that they have an identifiable essence - does not hold true of all things. In claiming that Heidegger's account of the sublime is superior to those of earlier thinkers, Young implies that there is an essence of the sublime, much like there is an essence of the square. Furthermore, Young seems to know what this essence is and to be capable of judging the extent to which Heidegger and others have succeeded in discovering it. It would seem more historically sensitive to say that the differences among various accounts of the sublime reflect different historical and philosophical contexts. The sublime is bound to play a different role and be understood differently from antiquity to the nineteenth century to the present. This is not to deny that the feeling of the sublime is something beyond the accounts that different thinkers have provided of it. The way I see it, philosophical reflections on the sublime draw on a genuine experience of feeling that has been shared by many people in different contexts and across time. The question arises, then, of how best to investigate this experience. Rather than proceed a priori, why not use the tools of psychology and other disciplines to investigate the feeling empirically?

Another approach is offered by the psychologist Vladimir J. Konečni, some of whose empirical studies we shall examine in a later chapter.

Konečni is interested in the phenomenon of aesthetic awe, powerful responses to great works of art and extraordinary natural phenomena. He sees such "extreme" responses as deserving serious inquiry, and argues that aesthetic awe deserves to be counted among the small number of fundamental emotions. Such responses, he contends, have likely occurred since primeval times, initially in response to unexpectedly encountered natural wonders.

An important aspect of Konečni's project is the attempt to remedy the conceptual, methodological and terminological confusions and obscurities that he sees as afflicting much research and writing on musical and aesthetic emotions. Hence the term "sublime" is reserved to describe objects, and "aesthetic awe" is the prototypical subjective reaction to a sublime stimulus. Being "touched" or "moved" (used interchangeably) are lesser responses. While these feelings always accompany aesthetic awe, there are many instances of being moved or touched that do not reach the "more profound, exhilarating, and elevating" state of aesthetic awe. As Konečni writes, "Being moved is a serious matter and it cannot be cheaply induced." He argues that music can be sublime, that is, capable of inducing aesthetic awe, only when it is "colossal" - possessing certain structural features and performed in vast and beautiful architectural spaces with excellent acoustics. In addition, a significant personal associative context is required, including associations conditioned and reinforced since childhood.

Despite the differences between us, I see my own project as complementary to Konečni's. I am interested in the full range of aesthetic responses that he describes - from being moved or touched all the way to the most rarefied states of aesthetic awe. However, while a philosopher can only applaud attempts to introduce conceptual and terminological clarity where it is lacking, I fear that some of Konečni's efforts here may be in vain. As I mentioned earlier, "sublime" has described both certain external objects and the internal states that they provoke from the earliest uses of the term through contemporary practice. Clearly, those who have thought deeply about these issues see continuity between sublime objects and the sublime mental states they induce. It will be interesting to consider why this is the case; conserving the terminological link between external object and internal mental state may help us to do so.

There is another reason why I prefer to use "sublime" to denote a larger range of phenomena and responses than Konečni sees prudent to allow. I do not want to have to decide, at the outset, which musical works and performances are "really" sublime. That is a task for music critics. Similarly, my permissive attitude removes the need to decide which listeners' subjective states attain full aesthetic awe and which reflect lesser states. Until there are reliable objective measures of these states such decisions are better set aside. As to whether or not being moved can be "cheaply induced," I believe that we should wait to examine the evidence rather than decide the matter by fiat at the outset. Again, to do otherwise may excessively narrow our inquiry; considering less dramatic responses to music that is less than awe-inspiring may eventually help us understand the most exalted responses to the greatest works.

* * *

To anticipate my conclusions: Rousseau distinguished between music's physical action and its moral action; that is, between its effect on the body as a series of mechanical vibrations and its symbolic significance as a culturally specific sign. These two ways of understanding music retain their importance today and inform research on the emotional power of music.

The answer to the mystery of music's power over human emotion is not to be found in the nature of music as a physical causal agent on the brain or body, although it will become evident that certain structural features of music do seem to have direct physical effects. Powerful responses to music are related to individual psychology, but cannot be reduced to the psychological peculiarities of those who undergo such responses. Quite general claims can be made about the type of music which provokes these responses, and even about specific musical works. General claims can also be made about the listeners who report such responses. These responses are not merely socially or culturally conditioned, although social and cultural norms, musical traditions, even history and philosophy, will each play a part. Finally, answers will not reside in music "itself" or in its beauty or expressiveness.

Music is *per hypothesis* indispensable to these responses, but no music is a sufficient cause of a powerful emotional response. All of these factors - music as a physical causal agent, music as an object of aesthetic contemplation, listeners as discrete individuals and listeners as members of a specific musical culture - are important, but in different respects and to different degrees. The account I propose rests on the nature of music as a human social practice and the nature of aesthetic value. Ultimately, the question of why some music tends to arouse experiences of the sublime in some listeners cannot be separated from the question of why any music at all matters to anyone.

In chapter 2 we take a closer look at some of the philosophical views that have influenced the way we now listen to music. These include ideas both about the nature of music and about appropriate emotional responses to music. To do so, we need to consider changes and continuities in the conception of the sublime, from its roots in antiquity through the early twentieth century.

2

HISTORY: MUSIC GIVES VOICE
TO THE INEFFABLE

THE IDEA THAT MUSIC might be capable of overcoming listeners and subverting their reason has a long history. These powerful emotional responses to music would seem to be cross-cultural and to have existed throughout history, if we accept the testimony of many different listeners in various cultures over long periods of time. But the precise way in which these strong responses have been interpreted, and the different forms that such responses take, depend on listeners' presence in a specific historical and philosophical culture. Each instance of music appreciation takes place within a certain context. Most obvious is the physical context - a listener may be alone in a darkened room, one of hundreds sitting quietly in a concert hall or an active participant in a ritual. Less obvious but just as important is the cultural or social context of the listening. What value does the listener's culture or sub-culture place on the particular work she hears and on the activity of listening to music more generally? What expectations and attitudes have in turn developed in the listener?

A culture's attitude towards music and towards particular works is informed by more general values and ideas, including religious beliefs, philosophy and conceptions of artistic merit. The fact that most listeners might not be aware of the particular philosophical doctrines that inform their experience of music does not make the ideas in question any less influential. To offer just one illustration - Handel was the first composer to be considered a genius by his contemporaries. Of course, there were musical geniuses before Handel; yet it was only in the eighteenth century that composers came to be considered artists rather than craftsmen and philosophers developed the theory of artistic genius. Both of these ideas needed to be in place before any composer could be considered a genius.

The western philosophical tradition of the sublime represents one such philosophical and cultural background against which a certain (large) group of listeners has experienced and interpreted their responses, and against which they continue to do so. Although there has been sublime music probably for as long as there has been music, music was not generally considered to be sublime until the late eighteenth century. The idea that music could be sublime goes hand-in-hand with two related convictions, both of which represent considerable philosophical and cultural transformations: first, the idea that instrumental music is superior to music with words; and second, the idea that instrumental music itself, without words, could be a vehicle of ideas. These changes in the conception of music occurred towards the end of the eighteenth century and they in turn inspired changes in the way audiences were expected to listen and respond. In this chapter we explore some of the philosophical background behind these changing conceptions of music. Just how did it come about that some music could be judged sublime or give rise to experiences of the sublime?

The first composer to be widely recognized as a creator of sublime works was Beethoven. His music is described as sublime with what one commentator has called "boring regularity." The "canonization" of Beethoven as a creative genius was largely the work of two men - the writer and critic E. T. A. Hoffmann and the composer Richard Wagner. Both responded to the philosophy of Immanuel Kant, but in different ways. Wagner's writings on Beethoven were also heavily influenced by the work of the philosopher Arthur Schopenhauer, who also was influenced by Kant. But before we delve into Kant's philosophy and its influence later in the nineteenth century, we need to take a step back and consider the history of the sublime more generally. How is it that the major exemplars of the sublime go from being mountains, waterfalls and thunderstorms in the eighteenth century, to operas, symphonies and string quartets by the late nineteenth century? Why did instrumental music gain its newfound prestige? How did attitudes to music and listeners' expectations of it change as a result?

THE SUBLIME IN ANTIQUITY

The modern history of the sublime begins in 1674 with the translation by Nicolas Boileau of Longinus' treatise *Peri Hupsous* ("On the Impressiveness of Style" in English, "De Sublimitate" in Latin). "Longinus" (as he is called by convention) was an otherwise unknown rhetorician of the first century CE. Some speculate that he was a hellenized Jew in the circle around Philo of Alexandria. There are long-standing debates as to what *Peri Hupsous* is fundamentally about, as "the sublime" is never explicitly defined. The quality of the sublime is variously associated with a text (or other object of contemplation), an author and the impact transmitted to an audience. Although Longinus' primary concern is the art of persuasion, he also makes provocative remarks on the sublime and nature, and the sublime and the fine arts. Perhaps because of his influence on seventeenth- and eighteenth-century literature and aesthetics, Longinus often seems like a contemporary. Indeed, one commentator finds a "strong Kantian ring" in many of his remarks.

Longinus writes that the sublime "consists in a certain loftiness and excellence of language." Sublime passages always please, and please all readers. In reading or hearing sublime language, we feel our souls "lifted up," and it may be difficult or even impossible to turn our attention away. Sublime language may even kindle terror in the breast of readers. Indeed, the rhetorician Hyperides is said *not* to be sublime because he rouses no emotion in the reader, certainly never terror. Most importantly, the sublime convinces through an appeal to the reader's heart, not his head: "A lofty passage does not convince the reason of the reader, but takes him out of himself. That which is admirable ever confounds our judgement, and eclipses that which is merely reasonable or agreeable. To believe or not is usually in our own power; but the Sublime, acting with an imperious and irresistible force, sways every reader whether he will or no." This idea that the sublime subverts reason and takes us out of ourselves will remain constant in later discussions.

Just as noble and lofty language appeals to human beings, so too does what is grand and majestic in nature: "whatever is useful or needful lies easily within man's reach; but he keeps his homage for what is astounding." Longinus writes that we admire great rivers such as the Nile, the Danube and the Rhine much more than we do streams; the ocean is even more impressive. Such scenes have a hold on us because of our very nature as human beings. Implanted in our souls is an "invincible yearning" for all that is great and more divine than ourselves.

For Longinus, the paradigm examples of the sublime are literature and nature. Yet it is worth taking a look at what he says about two other fine arts: sculpture and music. Longinus recognized that his praise of sublimity did not fit well with the aesthetic principles of his own day. He agrees that it would be inappropriate to prefer the "huge disproportioned" Colossus to a highly praised statue of the time, Polycletus' Doryphorus (The Spear-Bearer). The latter statue embodies an ideal of physical perfection; its proportions later became the standard for sculptors. We admire the Doryphorus more than the Colossus because in art we esteem exactness, and in nature magnificence. However, Longinus sees rhetoric as fundamentally different from sculpture and the other arts. Since we derive the faculty of speech from nature, our response to rhetoric and the appropriate aesthetic standards for it are closely akin to those appropriate for nature. That is why in statuary we admire close resemblance to the thing depicted, but in literature we require something that "transcends" humanity. Longinus' brief remarks on music give the impression that he regards it as being more like rhetoric than sculpture. In his discussion of how verbal composition can contribute to sublimity, he makes a direct comparison with music. This is worth quoting at length:

> harmony is an instrument which has a natural power, not only to win and to delight, but also in a remarkable degree to exalt the soul and sway the heart of man. When we see that a flute [*aulos*] kindles certain emotions in its hearers, rendering them almost beside themselves and full of an orgiastic frenzy, and that

by starting some kind of rhythmical beat it compels him who listens to move in time and assimilate his gestures to the tune, even though he has no taste whatever for music; when we know that the sounds of a harp, which in themselves have no meaning, by the change of key, by the mutual relation of the notes, and their arrangement in symphony, often lay a wonderful spell on an audience - though these are mere shadows and spurious imitations of persuasion, not, as I have said, genuine manifestations of human nature - can we doubt that composition (being a kind of harmony of that language which nature has taught us, and which reaches, not our ears only, but our very souls)...gains a complete mastery over our minds?

Although Longinus' main concern in this passage is language, we see here much in keeping with traditional ancient Greek attitudes to music. Music has power over the soul and body of listeners, including reluctant listeners. The arrangement of tones in a certain order according to a rhythmic pattern can be profoundly affecting. Music played on certain instruments can even be responsible for bringing about "orgiastic frenzy" or trance states. However, music lacks semantic meaning and so does not appeal to what is genuinely human in us. Interestingly, music would seem to be a more obvious exemplar of the sublime than linguistic composition, as the sublimity of composition is explained through the sublimity of music, not vice versa. Is music, then, a "false sublime"? That is, does it fail to merit listeners' sometimes powerful responses? Does a strong reaction to music say more about the listener than about the music that prompts it? These questions will remain with us.

THE SUBLIME IN
THE EIGHTEENTH CENTURY

The eighteenth century has been called a "Copernican Revolution" in aesthetics. This is because the question of whether an object is beautiful or sublime comes to depend on the experience of the spectator rather than the properties of the object itself. The most noticeable change among British writers was the shift away from a metaphysical approach in favour of psychology and introspection, likely due to the influence of John Locke's *An Essay Concerning Human Understanding* (1690). The next thinker to play an important role in the development of the sublime was Edmund Burke. When he published *A Philosophical Enquiry into the Origin of our Ideas of the Sublime and Beautiful* (1757), Longinus had been a direct influence on English criticism for not quite a hundred years.

Burke is resolutely sensationist. In other words, all that we can know is discovered through sensory experience and an analysis of it. While Longinus had focused on rhetoric and other sublime objects, Burke proposes a close examination of subjective human passions. Specifically, he sought the efficient cause of beauty and sublimity; that is, those states of the mind that cause changes in the body, or those properties of bodies that work a change in the mind. Besides his thoroughgoing empiricism, Burke's writings on the sublime are innovative in two main ways: his insistence on the connection between sublimity and terror, and his disjunction between beauty and the sublime. According to Burke, the major source of the sublime is terror; more precisely, it is those things which prompt the ideas of pain and danger. Terror, when it does not press too closely, always produces delight. The highest degree of the sublime is astonishment; admiration, reverence and respect are weaker forms. The feeling of "delightful horror" is said to be the most genuine effect and surest indication of the sublime. While there is an element of danger in many of the objects that arouse feelings of the sublime - for example, in thunderstorms and the raging sea - it is questionable to give terror the central place that Burke does. There are many sublime objects that are not frightening, or would only seem frightening to a very active imagination!

Burke's sensationism and commitment to empirical explanations can be seen in his discussion of the sublimity of sounds. Excessive loudness can fill the soul with terror, as can the sudden beginning or cessation of a loud sound. This is because when a sound is perceived, the ear is struck by a single pulse of air which makes the eardrum and inner ear vibrate according to the character of the stroke. If the stroke is strong, the ear can be subject to a considerable degree of tension. If the stroke is repeated, the listener expects a further repetition, and this expectation also becomes a source of tension. After a number of strokes the listener expects more, yet cannot predict exactly when they will come; the "surprise" when the strokes do arrive further increases the tension. The tension caused by the strokes to the ear, the expectation and the surprise can reach such a level as to be brought just to the threshold of pain. This tension is the source of the feeling of the aural sublime. We can see that the feeling of the sublime arises primarily through the action of sound on the nervous system; the operation of the mind (in expectation and surprise) is secondary.

Burke is convinced that the ideas of the beautiful and the sublime are frequently and improperly confused. He charges that even Longinus had made this mistake and inappropriately put together "things extremely repugnant to each other" under the name of the sublime. Burke was the first to insist on a clear-cut distinction between the beautiful and the sublime, and this would seem to be related to his conviction that the major source of the sublime is terror. (While it is possible to imagine a beautiful thing that is also terrible - perhaps a magnificent flower, one sniff of which will cause a quick and excruciating death - we do not typically associate beauty with fear.) For Burke the most important difference between the beautiful and the sublime is that the former is founded on pleasure, and the latter on pain. While the sublime causes astonishment, beauty causes love. Although the sublime and the beautiful may be found together, it does not follow that they are "in any way allied." Another major theme in the *Enquiry* is that the influence of reason on our passions has been overestimated. More often than not it is our ignorance of things that arouses emotion. Burke is perhaps at his most Longinian in his analysis of the power of the sublime over our reason. In states of astonishment (the highest form of the sublime) all of the motions of the soul are suspended. The mind is entirely filled with the sublime object to the extent that it cannot think of anything else and cannot even think coherently about the object in question. The power of the sublime is such that it "anticipates our reasonings" and carries us along "by an irresistible force."

In Britain Burke's writings on aesthetics had little influence on contemporary philosophers and critics interested in similar issues;

in particular, most rejected his strict sensationism. However, Burke's influence on writers and artists, and particularly on those interested in nature, was profound. His work helped to spread the cult of Romantic horror in the pre-Romantic period. As one commentator puts it, Burke's *Enquiry* "gave currency to a new complex of ideas which proved more influential than the theory on which it was based." The influence of Burke's *Enquiry* begins around the mid-1700s with the growth of interest in mountain scenery, and arguably continues into the present.

The musical culture of Burke's eighteenth century was in many ways different from our own. "Did People Listen in the 18th Century?" asks the title of an article in the scholarly journal *Early Music*. Many who have studied the musical history and concert-going behaviour of the period would answer with a resounding no. Audiences on the whole did not seem to pay serious and sustained attention to the performances they attended. The range of "appropriate" behaviour during a concert was much wider than it is today. Now, the words "classical" or "serious" music contain a set of nuances unimagined in the eighteenth century. Audience members were known to arrive late, leave early, rise from their seats to greet friends and chat during the performance. Opera was assumed to be accessible to all, and those who had attended the same opera many times felt no obligation to remain silent durng its performance. Mozart, in a letter to his father about his Paris concerts, proudly mentioned that the audience applauded during a particularly effective passage in the first movement of his symphony 31 in D major (the *"Paris" Symphony*). Mozart was gratified by their response and thought it entirely natural. (Incidentally, today no one is quite sure which passage it was that the Paris audience liked so much, as Mozart did not specify.)

Today, clapping between two movements is likely to be met with icy stares or condescension, to say nothing of clapping while the music is in progress! There is a great and understandable tendency to take the practices of one's own culture and historical milieu as normative. But this tendency must be resisted if we are to understand other cultures or our own historical past. The principles adhered to by "serious" listeners today were not firmly in place until after 1850. In trying to understand the changes in the significance of music from the early nineteenth century until the present we would have to take account of a number of different factors. These include: the growth of cities; changes in modes of transport; advances in the measurement of time; developments in science and technology; changing attitudes to the natural world; and economic and demographic changes. These went hand-in-hand with developing attitudes to music and changing expectations of listeners.

But by the end of the eighteenth century attitudes to music, and in particular to instrumental music, were beginning to change. Many of these changes can be traced to changes in the philosophy of art and in the growing emergence of a "system" of the arts. Before the end of the eighteenth century, music theory had been profoundly influenced by models of language and rhetoric. The task of the composer was to reach the audience, much like that of the orator. Music without a text was seen as vague and imprecise. Within less than a generation, the "vagueness" of instrumental music would come to be seen as one of its virtues and many would consider music to be the highest of the arts. These changes were being slowly prepared by various debates throughout the eighteenth century and would reach their culmination in later Romantic thinkers. To understand these changes, we need to turn to the philosophy of Immanuel Kant.

KANT ON MUSIC AND ON THE SUBLIME

Almost everyone who writes on Kant's contributions to the philosophy of music feels compelled to disclose at the outset that Kant seems to have had little affinity for art in general and for music in particular. His preferences ran to loud and boisterous military music, heroic fanfares and large orchestras, and he is said not to have cared for solo instruments in the least. In his major work on aesthetics, the *Critique of Judgement* (the *Third Critique* as it is sometimes called), he disdainfully compares music to perfume, because both extend their influence further than is desired. Indeed, it is said that Kant once wrote indignantly to the director of police, demanding that he prevent the inmates of a nearby prison from singing hymns. Kant's contribution to understanding aesthetic experience has nevertheless been immense, and an examination of it is necessary fully to understand many contemporary issues in philosophical aesthetics. His *Critique of Judgement* is the work which, more than any other, defines the parameters and sets the problems for modern aesthetics. We shall first consider the main aspects of Kant's account of the sublime so that we can then compare it with Burke's account and draw out its relevance for music. It is known that Kant was familiar with Burke's *Enquiry* because he quotes from it in the *Critique of Judgement*. I have chosen to focus on this rather than on Kant's earlier work, *Observations on the Feeling of the Beautiful and Sublime*. Authors should be judged by their best work, and I think no one would disagree that the *Third Critique* is superior in this case. Also, the *Critique* proved to be much more influential than the *Observations*.

Kant's favourite illustrations of the sublime would already have been stock examples to his contemporary readers: mountains, the raging sea, the vast starry sky and violent weather patterns. Although natural phenomena are central to Kant's discussion of the sublime, he does not reject the idea that artefacts might also be considered sublime. Indeed, his discussion of the pyramids and St Peter's in Rome as examples of the sublime suggests that they might be. Kant focuses on the sublime in nature, as he believes that the sublime in art must adhere to the same conditions as the natural sublime. In fine art the beautiful and the sublime may be combined to form a tragedy in verse, a didactic poem or an oratorio. Tellingly for Kant, ideas can also be sublime. Burke, in keeping with his sensationism, pays little attention to the sublimity of ideas. In fact, he mentions only one idea as possibly productive of the sublime - the idea of bodily pain. Kant in contrast considers the command in the Hebrew Bible against graven images to be the most sublime passage in the Jewish Law. Later he conjectures that the most sublime thought ever expressed is the inscription on the Temple of Isis: "I am all that is and all that was and all that shall be, and no mortal hath lifted my veil." We shall see later that Kant's belief that ideas as well as objects could be sublime would be important for the development of Romantic attitudes to music.

For Kant, judgements of the sublime are related in a distinct way to our mental powers, as well as to our understanding of ourselves as rational beings, and especially (as we shall see) as *moral* rational beings. Kant distinguishes two types of judgements of the sublime: mathematical and dynamic. Natural objects are mathematically sublime if contemplation of them arouses the idea of infinity; that is, of an uncountable quantity. We can contemplate objects aesthetically and estimate their magnitude subjectively by mere intuition or measurement of the eye. In such cases we do not try to come to any numerical concept of how great the object is. For example, imagine contemplating a vast plain, stretching flat in all directions as far as the eye can see. We do not measure the plain according to definite standards or examine it with an idea in mind of what a plain should be like; we merely try to take in the vast space. The possibility of actually experiencing infinite space challenges the limits of the imagination, since anything infinite in Kant's sense would fall outside the scope of the laws of nature. Yet we can understand the *idea* of infinite space well enough. The mind enjoys the sense of its own power, and this feeling is the basis of judgements of the mathematically sublime.

In judgements of the dynamically sublime, the object or phenomenon in question is perceived as something mighty or powerful which has no power over us. Imagine watching and listening to a furious thunderstorm from the safety of your home. You realize that if the storm were a few miles closer, your house would risk being struck by lightning and burnt to the ground. This thought inspires feelings of fear and anxiety - the negative component of the feeling of the sublime. The realization that you are safe at home and out of immediate danger is also necessary for the experience of the sublime, but it is not the immediate reason for that experience. Rather, the feeling of the sublime is ultimately founded on the respect you have for nature as a superior force, combined with the realization that a part of you is "super-sensible" - not subject to natural laws and thus potentially self-governing, unlike nature. Judgements of the sublime require culture, even more so than judgements of the beautiful. What Kant has in mind is that without the development of moral ideas, those large and powerful objects which arouse judgements of the sublime would be merely terrible and would lack any positive attraction.

Kant was much influenced by Burke's idea that the beautiful and the sublime are fundamentally distinct. For Kant, the beautiful is connected with the form of an object, while the sublime may also be found in formless objects. The sublime is simply incompatible with charm, but the attractive or alluring aspects of a beautiful object can add to our appreciation of it. Like Burke, Kant is convinced that judgements of the beautiful and the sublime have different causal histories and a different subjective feeling to those who experience them. Although the beautiful and the sublime are both based in the feeling of pleasure and both please in themselves, the type of pleasure each offers is different. Judgements of the beautiful are purely pleasurable, but judgements of the sublime contain an element of unease mingled with pleasure. The mind is alternately attracted and repelled by the sublime object. Kant described the sublime as "that which is terrible to sensibility and yet is attractive." The pleasure we take in the sublime is thus most accurately characterized for Kant as a feeling of admiration or respect. He famously pronounced it a "negative pleasure."

While Burke and Kant seem to agree that the feeling of the sublime is not unambiguously pleasurable, Kant's description of the negative feelings aroused by the sublime is much more nuanced. Recall that for Burke the sublime is aroused by feelings of terror, as long as the terror is not too proximate. For Kant, it is enough that we *recognize* that nature is fearful for it to be the object of a judgement of the sublime; we do not actually have to *experience* terror or fear. Kant claims that the feeling of the sublime is caused by the feeling of "a momentary checking of the vital powers and a consequent stronger outflow of them." This sounds more like discomfort, perhaps followed by exhilaration, than what we normally think of as pain. The pain in judgements of the sublime is, for Kant, at the same time "purposive." Perhaps an appropriate physical analogy for Kant's mental pain would be the soreness one feels after an invigorating workout or game of squash - somewhat unpleasant, but nothing so debilitating as the pain of (say) kidney stones.

The greatest difference between Kant and Burke is rooted in the differences in the projects they undertake. Burke's approach to the feeling of the sublime is resolutely empirical and physiological. He thus continues the "Copernican Revolution" in aesthetics with his focus on the mind of the experiencing individual, rather than the aesthetic object. He seeks out those states of the mind that cause changes in the body, or those properties of bodies that work a change in the mind. Kant's well-known critique of such approaches is that if judgements of taste are inter-subjectively valid, then they must be based on a principle that is itself outside of experience. This requirement leads Kant to the paradoxical claim that what is properly sublime is the human mind, not the large or powerful object viewed by any particular individual. In judgements of the mathematical sublime, what is sublime is the mind's awareness of its own power. In judgements of the dynamic sublime, what is sublime is the realization that the will is potentially autonomous. In both cases, wild or majestic nature is called "sublime" because it is an occasion for the mind to recognize its *own* sublimity. Kant has thus completed the "Revolution": not only is the human viewer the proper locus of aesthetic investigation, but she is also the genuine cause of certain aesthetic judgements.

CHANGING CURRENTS

We have now uncovered two of the key ideas that needed to be in place before music without a text could be considered sublime. First, there is the crucial underpinning provided by the eighteenth-century "Copernican Revolution" in aesthetics. That is, the experience of the spectator, rather than the properties of the object, determine whether something is beautiful or sublime. In the spirit, the perceiver in Kant's aesthetics is an active agent rather than a passive receiver. The second key idea is the belief that, in addition to mountains, waterfalls and cathedrals, ideas themselves could be sublime. The third key component needed before Romantic philosophers could crown music queen of the arts was the conviction that instrumental music could be the vehicle of ideas. Once it is accepted that music can convey thought and that ideas can be sublime, it is but a short step to the idea that music itself can be sublime, if only the active listener attends in the right way.

The full story of how music comes to be regarded as a vehicle of ideas is told in Mark Evan Bonds' *Music as Thought: Listening to the Symphony in the Age of Beethoven*. The importance of Kant's philosophy in these developments can hardly be overstated. As we have seen, Kant, personally and philosophically, was not sympathetic to music. However, his ideas were taken up by later thinkers who had greater interest in and appreciation of music. In particular, later thinkers were inspired by Kant's account of aesthetic ideas in the *Third Critique*. Unfortunately, these sections contain some of the most obscure passages in that book. Aesthetic ideas and rational ideas are counterparts, comparable to two sides of a coin. A *rational idea* is a concept of the mind to which no sensible intuition or representation of the imagination can be adequate. That is, a rational idea is one that cannot be adequately conveyed in words or pictures. Kant's example of a rational idea is the "kingdom of the blessed." Whatever awaits the righteous after death, no words or pictures can do it justice or convey it to us. An *aesthetic idea* is an imaginative representation - a kind of mental image - which brings about much thought, but to which no *single* definite thought or concept is commensurate. It is difficult to provide an example of an aesthetic idea, as they cannot be summed up or made intelligible by language. They are, in a sense, ineffable. According to Kant, poets (one is tempted to say creative artists more generally) try to express rational ideas using sensory means. That is, they try to give the appearance of objective reality to concepts, such as life after death, which lie beyond the bounds of experience. Or, if the artist deals with things of which experience is possible - human emotion, aspects of nature, etc. - he tries to present these things with a "completeness" they lack in the ordinary course of nature. In order to do this artists have to work with aesthetic ideas.

Closely linked to aesthetic ideas are aesthetic attributes. These are forms which artists use to make us think of rational ideas. An example is helpful here: "The act of divine creation" is a rational idea which is not given in experience. No human being was present at the creation of the world. Michelangelo tried to evoke or "realize to sense" this rational idea in his well-known fresco where two outstretched fingers - God's and Adam's - are about to touch. The aesthetic ideas expressed by the fresco - impossible to convey adequately in language - might include God's benevolence and wisdom, the fundamentally dependent and contingent nature of human life and the perfection of divine design. The aesthetic attribute by which these ideas are evoked is the form of Michelangelo's fresco; that is, the perceptual qualities inherent in it (the fresco's colours, shapes and textures) and their relations to one another, as perceived by a subject. The aesthetic attributes are at most approximate imaginative representations. It is important to note that they do not simply present given concepts. These concepts, as rational ideas, cannot be adequately represented; or, if they are the sorts of things that we can have experience of, our experience of them is necessarily incomplete. Instead, the aesthetic attributes "furnish" aesthetic ideas. This means that they engage and enliven the mind by alerting it to the possibility of an unlimited range of related representations. A really effective work of art is thus one whose meaning is not readily exhausted. We keep finding more things to say about it, and more connections to make between it and other things. Kant's own examples of aesthetic attributes are unfortunately not very illuminating. "The king of heaven" is a rational idea; the aesthetic attribute that expresses it is Jupiter's eagle with lightning in its talons. By way of further explication he analyses a poem by Frederick the Great which many subsequent commentators have found notable only for its banality.

This idea that art might express truth that language could not was to become a cornerstone of the Romantic Movement. Kant indicated that music could express aesthetic ideas, but it was left to others to develop and apply his insights. One of the most influential thinkers to take up his ideas and apply them to music was the German writer, critic and composer E. T. A. Hoffmann. Today he is perhaps best remembered as the author of the story on which Tchaikovsky's *Nutcracker* is based. His 1810 review of Beethoven's Fifth Symphony has been called arguably "the single most important and influential work of music criticism ever written" and it was the central document in the reception of Beethoven's music in the composer's lifetime. Hoffmann contrasted the "transcendent" Beethoven with the "innocent" Haydn and "ethereal" Mozart. Virtually all subsequent histories of music covering the eighteenth and nineteenth centuries followed this template. Hoffmann was among the first to link the three composers, and the first to declare Beethoven the greatest of them. The review was very widely read and the principles it expressed were taken up into the most basic assumptions about music and how to listen to it.

Hoffmann's review is shot through with the aesthetics of the sublime, although he hardly uses the word "sublime." First, there is the association of instrumental music - Beethoven's music in particular - with the infinite. The phrase "infinite longing" is repeated several times. The "sole subject" of instrumental music is said to be the infinite. Beethoven's Fifth Symphony leads the listener "forward in a climax that climbs up and up into the spirit world of the infinite." His music opens us to the realm of the "colossal" and "immeasurable," and we perceive "giant shadows surging back and forth." Recall that for Kant one form of the sublime - the mathematical sublime - was summoned by objects that arouse the idea of the infinite. Next, in a contention inspired as much by Burke as by Kant, Hoffman claims that Beethoven's music is not unambiguously beautiful or pleasurable. The listener is "powerless to step out of that wondrous spirit world where pain and pleasure embrace him in the form of sound." Beethoven's music is said to move the levers of fear, horror, terror and pain. Finally, the power of instrumental music is contrasted with the limitations of language. Hoffman declares that the "magic" of music was so strong that it had to break the chains that bound it to another art - poetry. Words can express "mere earthly pleasures" but deep souls seek a "higher expression," such as can be found in instrumental music. In speaking of deep mysterious things one must use sublime and glorious language. Hoffmann sums up these thoughts with a poetic image that recalls the passage in the *Critique of Judgement* where Kant claims that the inscription on the Temple of Isis was the most sublime thought ever expressed: "The dance of the priests of Isis will always be an exultant hymn."

How do listeners figure in all of this? Certainly, Hoffmann expected music to arouse listeners, even possibly to overpower them. But the rhetorical model, in which it is the composer's task to reach listeners, no longer applies. Instead, it is the job of listeners to understand composers. What of listeners who were bewildered or left numb by Beethoven's music, rather than appreciative? Hoffman would have them work harder: "Could it be *your* fault that you do not understand the master's language as the initiated understand it, so that the portals of the inmost sanctuary remain closed to you?" he asked. Here we may have an origin of the idea that we have to be good enough for art, and not vice versa. One scholar of the period considers the "open scorn" that Hoffmann heaped on readers to be itself "no small milestone" in the history of musical aesthetics. Indeed, its echoes reach down to our own day.

Hoffmann's writings were among the first to take up Kantian themes and apply them to music, and in particular to the "sublime" music of Beethoven. The work of the philosopher Arthur Schopenhauer (1788-1860), also inspired by Kant, would be similarly important in the consolidation of Beethoven's status as an artistic genius. We shall see that Schopenhauer himself was both greatly influenced by Kant and sharply critical of him. I have so far only hinted at the importance to our inquiry of Schopenhauer. The list of writers and artists directly influenced by his work is extremely impressive - Richard Wagner, Gustav Mahler, Thomas Mann, Joseph Conrad, Leo Tolstoy, Henry James and Thomas Hardy, to mention only the best known. The philosopher Bryan Magee has conjectured that the influence of Schopenhauer on the creative artists of the very first rank surpasses that of any other philosopher since his time and perhaps that of any other philosopher since the ancient Greeks. Schopenhauer's views on music have also greatly contributed to the culture and practice of classical or art music appreciation.

In his seminal work, the *Critique of Pure Reason*, Kant had distinguished between the world of phenomena or appearance (what we can see, hear, touch, taste and smell) and the world of noumena or things-in-themselves (things as they really are). Although the noumena somehow underlie the phenomenal world we cannot know them; we have no perceptual access to them. Schopenhauer accepts this distinction between the world as it appears and the world of things-in-themselves, but makes some important changes. Most notably, he identifies the world of noumena with the Will. We can glimpse the Will when we consider our own volition and bodily movements. Through introspection, we can come to realize that our entire inner nature is one of willing or striving. Schopenhauer's notorious pessimism has its roots in this conception of our inner nature. The Will constantly seeks satisfaction and repose which are ultimately attainable only in death. Experiencing beauty in nature or works of art is one way we can temporarily escape the tyranny of the Will. In ordinary, everyday perception our faculty of knowledge is a servant of the Will. However, in aesthetic perception disinterest is possible; we can (and should) set aside practical cares when we contemplate objects that have aesthetic value. When we consider an object for its own sake in this way, knowledge can be briefly independent of the Will. We glimpse the true nature of reality and experience ourselves as the "*pure* will-less, painless, timeless *subject of knowledge*." Thus in aesthetic perception, the perceiver becomes one with the act of perception.

Like Kant, Schopenhauer posited a distinction between the beautiful and the sublime; although there are similarities in their accounts the differences are significant. Recall that Kant conceptualized the beautiful and the sublime as distinct forms of judgement. Schopenhauer has a broader (and ultimately more satisfying) conception of the beautiful than did Kant and he makes it clear that sublime objects are also beautiful. Hence the sublime is best seen as a sub-class of the beautiful. According to Schopenhauer, beautiful objects "invite" aesthetic contemplation and reward it with pleasure. Knowledge overcomes the Will without a struggle. Yet certain beautiful objects are at the same time "hostile"; that is, they pose a threat. In these cases, the beholder understands the danger he may be in, but consciously turns away from it, giving himself up entirely to will-less knowledge. The state of pure knowing is achieved only with "a conscious and violent tearing away." The resulting state of exaltation, when the beholder is elevated above himself and above willing more generally and may quietly contemplate those very objects so terrible to the Will, is the feeling of the sublime.

We saw earlier that for Kant judgements of the sublime were inter-subjectively valid because of their moral underpinning. There is a reason why all cognitively normal and encultured adults find the same things sublime. It is our very nature as "super-sensible" - not subject to the laws of nature and hence potentially autonomous - that makes such judgements possible. Schopenhauer rejects this connection between the moral and the aesthetic. Consequently, aesthetic judgements do not have the same claim to inter-subjective validity that they had in Kant and are much more liable to vary with the psychology of individual perceivers. Consequently, Schopenhauer claims that those whose imagination is not great or who lack aesthetic sensitivity may not respond to more subtle examples of the sublime.

A striking difference between the aesthetics of Kant and Schopenhauer is their relative evaluations of music. Very much of the eighteenth century, Kant considers music without a text to have no cognitive content, and vacillates on the question of whether music is one of the fine arts. Schopenhauer's attitude could not be more different. He is convinced that music can reveal the inner nature of reality. The other art-forms represent the world; music, as it is non-representational, cannot represent anything. Instead it is a copy of the Will itself or "willing made audible". Thus nature (the phenomenal world) and music are together two different yet parallel expressions of the same thing. The reason why music has such a "powerful and penetrating" effect is because of its status as a copy of the Will. Recall that the only form of music that Kant mentions as a possible source of the sublime is an oratorio - music with a text. Again, Schopenhauer's position is radically different. While music (in song) can "enter into a relationship" with poetry, the text must never dominate. Words accompanying music are "a foreign extra of secondary value" and the effect of the tones themselves is incomparably more powerful and rapid than that of words.

THE LATE NINETEENTH CENTURY AND BEYOND

Richard Wagner first read Schopenhauer in late 1854; only a few years later he was probably the philosopher's most fervent disciple in Germany. Schopenhauer's influence on Wagner can hardly be overstated. Perhaps most strikingly, the relationship between music and words in Wagner's operas is transformed. In the operas written after his assimilation of Schopenhauer, it can be difficult to hear the singing over the instrumental music at times. It has been said that the sheer weight of orchestral sound is "unprecedented." Wagner's 1870 essay on Beethoven is the central document of his reception of Schopenhauer. Large sections of it consist of quotations, paraphrases and exegesis of Schopenhauer's major work, *The World as Will and Representation*. Wagner was convinced that Beethoven was the first composer whose music revealed to the world "that deepest mystery of music"; that is, the first composer whose music exemplified Schopenhauer's philosophy of music. The state of both musicians and composers is described in terms highly reminiscent of the sublime, although the word itself is not used. A few examples will make this clear:

> This prodigious breaking down the floodgates of appearance must necessarily call forth in the inspired musician a state of ecstasy wherewith no other can compare ... One state surpasses his, and one alone - the saint's ...

> The dreamlike nature of the state into which we thus are plunged through sympathetic hearing - ...

> And in truth it is in this state alone that we immediately belong to the musician's world. From out that world, which nothing else can picture, the musician casts the meshwork of his tones to net us, so to speak; or, with his wonder-drops of sound he dews our brain as if by magic, and robs it of the power of seeing aught save our own inner world.

We find here many similarities between earlier descriptions of sublime experiences and the effect of music. The musician (and presumably attentive listeners also) experience "ecstasy" and "dreamlike" states - clearly subversions of rationality, if not altered states of consciousness. Music transports listeners to a heightened state; it works on our brains "as if by magic" and compels us to look within. This avowal of music's power comes hand in hand with certain expectations regarding the listening experience. Listeners could legitimately expect to be transported, and these experiences would heighten their concert-going experience.

By the end of the nineteenth century Schopenhauer's name had become a "comfortable reference point" in intellectual discourse. He was also the most widely read and influential philosopher in Vienna in the 1890s. I have already mentioned that his influence on Wagner is evident in the latter's essay on Beethoven, an important document for the growing cult of Beethoven as genius. We can perhaps also see his influence in Gustav Mahler's championing of the works of Wagner and Mozart. (Mahler gave the collected works of Schopenhauer as a Christmas present to the composer Bruno Walter in 1894.) As director of the Imperial Opera, Mahler was substantially responsible for their rapidly growing popularity.

Schopenhauer's influence can be discerned in more abstract ways as well. Briefly, changes in music and in habits of listening can be traced back to him and to those he influenced. During Burke's time it seemed without doubt that vocal music was superior in every way to instrumental. We have seen a similar prejudice in Kant for music with a text. By the mid-nineteenth-century revival of interest in Schopenhauer this traditional relationship between words and music had been completely disrupted. Instrumental music, not words, was now the primary vehicle of meaning and significance. Even one of Wagner's greatest detractors, the music critic Eduard Hanslick, accepts this reversal and treats texts as extraneous to the music. Just as music has been "freed" from accompanying texts, so too has it been liberated from the world of appearances more generally. Music must not attempt to represent the world but, through its expressive power, reveal the Will. Music exists as a world of its own, or rather, music voices aspects of the world that are otherwise inaccessible.

With the changes in music as an art came changes in the ways listeners approached music. These changes were not due only to music's enhanced status among the arts and the increased stature of certain composers. Listening to music now could give one access to a whole world; however, some ways of listening were better than others. An attitude of disinterest - setting aside one's personal and practical concerns - was of course necessary in order to experience music fully, but it was not sufficient. Remember that for Schopenhauer aesthetic experience is not democratic; only the sensitive will be able to discern the sublime in its more subtle manifestations. This places a burden on audiences to listen in the "right" way so as to hear the "right" things. To do less would be to risk being thought of as insensitive. It also repositions composers from the role of entertainers or courtiers to that of creative titans.

* * *

Our examination of music and the modern sublime has taken us from eighteenth-century Britain to late nineteenth-century Vienna. In that time music went from being of peripheral concern to philosophers of art to being absolutely central. Music itself went from being the servant of texts to inhabiting a world of its own, beyond mere words. With the changes in music came a new mode of listening - disinterested, contemplative, reverential. No doubt there are many reasons for these changes, including the development of bourgeois norms of social decorum and even the changing architecture of concert venues. Yet the philosophical factors I have pointed to - the responsibility of listeners to understand composers, the need for disinterested contemplation, the delineation of the sublime as a distinctive aesthetic response, the conviction that music can be a vehicle of ideas and might even be revelatory of the world as it truly is - should not be underestimated.

Throughout the history of writing on the sublime, sublime objects - whether they are mountains, sculptures or symphonies - are thought to bring about sublime responses in those who contemplate them. In the next chapter we take a closer look at sublime or emotionally strong responses to music. What does it feel like, from the inside, to be overpowered by music?

3

TEARS, CHILLS AND BROKEN BONES

THE GUESTS ASSEMBLE IN THE SALON AFTER DINNER.
Would they care to hear some music? Perhaps the pianist could play
Vinteuil's *Sonata in F sharp*? But the hostess, Proust's Mme Verdurin,
protests, admonishing her husband for even suggesting the piece: "No,
no, no, not my sonata!...I don't want to be made to cry until I get a cold
in the head, and neuralgia all down my face, like last time; thanks very
much, I don't intend to repeat that performance; you are all very kind
and considerate; it is easy to see that none of you will have to stay in bed,
for a week."

While they might not describe their responses to music in the same
way that Mme Verdurin does, many people have had similar experiences. In this chapter we shall read a number of first-hand descriptions of sublime or emotionally strong responses to music. Although
each response reflects the personality, background and musical taste
of the listener in question (just as Mme Verdurin's response reflects
her personality), there is more commonality among the descriptions
than you might expect. When the experiences differ, they tend to differ in specific respects. The listeners who have shared these descriptions give us an idea of what their strong emotional responses to music
can feel like from the inside. Examining this range of examples will
help those who have never experienced strong emotional responses
to music to understand what all the fuss is about. If you have had a
similar experience you will be able to compare it to the descriptions

here. Once we have considered a rich variety of these descriptions we shall be better able to understand the reasons why people respond to music as they do.

Where do these descriptions come from? Most have been collected by psychologists, in particular by Alf Gabrielsson and his team at Uppsala University, in Sweden. The SEM ("Strong Experiences of Music") Project has collected over a thousand descriptions of listening experiences from nearly nine hundred people. In these studies, volunteers were asked to describe, in their own words, "the strongest, most intense experience of music that you have ever had" in as much detail as possible, and to complete a supplementary questionnaire. Researchers made efforts to include listeners of both genders, different ages, occupations and musical preferences. Since the types of responses to music that we are interested in reflect only certain aspects of the "strong experiences of music" in the work of Gabrielsson and his team, I have been selective when drawing on their data. Of the remaining descriptions in this chapter, some are from autobiographical writings; a few have been reported to me personally; others are from literary sources.

This mixing of sources might seem indiscriminate. In particular, why examine both "genuine" and literary descriptions? One reason is the hope that professional writers whose stock-in-trade is description will be able to illuminate aspects of musical experience that less articulate non-professionals cannot. Also, it will be interesting to see just what kinds of differences and similarities we find between these two types of sources.

THREE (MORE OR LESS) TYPICAL DESCRIPTIONS

In this first account, reported to the SEM Project, the writer thinks back to an event that occurred when he was seventeen years old. Although a fan of Sibelius' *Finlandia*, he suspected that he would not be able to sit through the radio broadcast of the entire *Second Symphony*, a feeling about longer musical works that perhaps is shared by many! However, this listener was surprised by the profundity of his response to the music:

> I remember how the music penetrated my consciousness entirely. How I gradually lost contact with the ground and experienced an

ecstasy of all my senses. Yes, it wasn't only my hearing that received its share!

When the tremendous intensification of the finale started, I cried. I remember that my face was all wet, and I experienced a happiness that, as I realized later, only could be compared with an intense love of another person.

I was so totally moved and happy that I just had to sit down and write a letter to this fellow-being Jean [*sic*] Sibelius, thanking him for giving me and many others this incredible music, that seemed to purify oneself ... both physically and mentally.

The second description is from a *New Yorker* article written by John Seabrook. He describes the emotional climax ("the money note") in a performance by then up-and-coming pop singer Cherie:

Cherie hit the money note with full force - "When I cry I'm weak / I'm learning to *fly*." As her voice went up on "fly," an electric guitar came floating up with it, and the tone was so pure that a chill spread over my shoulders, prickling the skin.

Finally, the short-storywriter Robin Parks describes this experience in a letter to the art critic James Elkins:

I cried (so hard I had to leave) at a little concert where a young man played solo cello Bach suites. It was a weird little Methodist church and there were only about fifteen of us in the audience, the cellist alone on the stage. It was midday. I cried because (I guess) I was overcome with love. It was impossible for me to shake the sensation (mental, physical) that J.S. Bach was in the room with me, and I loved him.

One thing that should be evident immediately is that each of these three listeners describes *physical reactions* to the music - crying (in the first and the third) and chills (in the second). The vast majority of real-life descriptions I have read mention physical symptoms. Besides the fairly common reports of chills and crying, physical responses to music include shortness of breath, increase in heart rate, trembling, hair standing on end ("gooseflesh" - piloerection, more technically), pain in the chest or stomach, and (rarely) loss of consciousness. Reports of physical responses are less common in fictional or literary descriptions. (Although we should not forget Mme Verdurin, who says that listening to the andante of Vinteuil's Sonata "breaks every bone in my body.") One of the reasons for the presence of physical symptoms in real-life narratives is that they seem a clear marker of strong experience. A listener who is asked to describe a strong emotional response to music is likely to remember more vividly a time she cried, say, than a time when she did not. Their relative absence in fiction may be because professional writers have the skill to convey the depth of a character's response without actually stating that tears were shed, etc.

Physical responses to music are significant because they are clear indications that the music has overcome listeners and undermined their defences. Elkins, in his book on people who have cried in front of paintings, writes that tears show, without room for doubt, that *something* has happened: "They are witnesses."

A second significant feature of the two longer descriptions (the first and third) is the writer's report of *social (interpersonal) feelings and connections*, in both cases here to the composer of the work that is heard. The first writer describes his feelings for the music as comparable only to "intense love of another person" and feels gratitude towards Sibelius. The third describes "love" for Bach. As we consider more descriptions we shall see that reports of such feelings are nearly as common as reports of physical responses. Why should this be? Many people think of listening to music as anything but social. Music for them is an escape from the world and (sometimes) from other people, whether they listen at home alone, through headphones while packed into public transit or with their eyes closed, shutting out the rest of the audience at a concert. So how could it be that some of the strongest and deepest responses to music share a social or communal aspect? A fully worked-out answer to this will have to wait. For now, let us notice how common the response is.

These three accounts are different in many ways. Each is to a different musical genre - respectively twentieth-century symphonic, contemporary pop and solo baroque. The first and second are responses to recorded or broadcast music, the third to a live performance. (I do not know whether the first listener heard a live performance or a recording broadcast over the radio.) The first listener is alone, the second and third are with small groups. There is one major difference among these three accounts. While the first and third accounts seem to describe responses to long sections of music, the second describes a response to a specific local feature - the singer's leap in pitch. Is it legitimate to group them together, or are the first and third fundamentally different from the second? There are at least two possible explanations. First, in the first and third account (of the Sibelius and the Bach), the listener in fact responds to specific local features of the music. Either the authors failed to mention this, or they did not realize it at the time. A second possibility is that the author of the second description highlights the singer's jump in pitch, but failed to realize (or to mention) the larger musical construct (harmony, rhythm, timbre) which made possible his strong response to the leap in pitch. If either of these explanations is plausible, then the phenomena we are dealing with are similar enough to be grouped and studied together.

A third possibility is that chills and tears, while both physical responses, are fundamentally different and carry different signification for our investigation of strong emotional responses to music. Chills might seem to be more "visceral" and less subject either to prevailing social practices or to individual control. Sometimes we can successfully hold back tears, but can we really hold back a chill? However, chills are not a reflexive response any more than tears are. They too depend on the presence of certain conditions and the absence of inhibiting factors. They are no more an "automatic" response than are tears. Chills and tears, whether experienced in conjunction or separately, may indicate different things - about the music they are responses to or about the people who experience them - but (at this point) we can say that their differences are insignificant enough that we can study them together.

ADDITIONAL DESCRIPTIONS

Let us consider some additional descriptions of strong emotional responses to music. You may notice features we have already come across - physical reactions and the feeling of social connections. Both are present in this account by the philosopher Ted Bond. He describes listening to Adam Harasiewicz's recording of Chopin's *Nocturne in C sharp minor*, Op. 27, No. 1:

> I was very moved, touched, or whatever you want to call it. I trembled. I raised my hands and covered my face. I said aloud: "My God, how Harasievich brings out the agony in this music!" I felt tears coming on. Then I noticed the nervous calm in the music and the would-be brightening. This was just noticing; there was no call for an emotional response.

Bond's account is distinctive in that he notes a connection with a performer rather than a composer. This probably reflects his familiarity with the work; he is able to hear features specific to a particular performance and attribute them to the pianist rather than to the composer.

The next account of physical responses to music is particularly vivid. This anonymous volunteer to the SEM Project claims he had never "consciously" listened to classical music but had only heard it in the background. He was given a recording of Tchaikovsky's *Pathétique Symphony* by a friend, and listened to it out of "duty," anticipating boredom:

> Only a few bars of the symphony had been played when suddenly I felt a chilly sensation at the back of my neck. The hair at the back of my head seemed to begin growing, and the chilly sensation began travelling through my whole body. There was a thick lump in my stomach that seemed to slowly expand, the pain became so intense that I had to fold both my arms around my abdomen with the intention of preventing what appeared to be heading towards an internal explosion, and my breathing became difficult. I started to cry, and the more I did so the less the pain in my stomach became.

A feature found in this account and in many additional descriptions is the writer's *total absorption in the music*. This was also evident in the very first account quoted where the writer said that the music "penetrated my consciousness entirely." The following description is particularly rich for illustrating all three of the features we have so far discussed. Again, the listener reports his reactions to Tchaikovsky's *Pathétique Symphony* - a work frequently mentioned in connection with strong emotional responses:

> In certain passages it evokes sobs and I feel totally crushed - my listening is fully concentrated, and the rest of the world disappears in a way, and I become merged in the music or the music in me, it fills me completely. I also get physical reactions … wet eyes, a breathing that gets sobbing in certain passages, a feeling of crying in my throat and chest. Trying to find words for the emotions themselves, I would like to use words as: crushed, shaken, tragedy, maybe death, absorption, but also tenderness, longing, desire (vain), a will to live, prayer. The whole experience also has the character of a total standstill, a kind of meditative rest, a last definite and absolute end, after which nothing else can follow.
>
> One more thing is of special interest … It is something that has happened solely with the 'Pathétique' and not at all with any other music whatsoever. It is that I feel that I meet the composer! I think he communicates directly with me, and I think that I *know him personally!* I know who he is.

We can see here: total absorption in the music - the writer reports that "the rest of the world disappears in a way"; several different physical responses - tears, sobbing and difficulty breathing; and a feeling of social connection, again with the composer. The writer feels that he knows Tchaikovsky, who communicates with him directly.

Sometimes descriptions of being overcome and absorbed by music seem to border on trance states. Consider the following two accounts. The first writer describes a Mike Oldfield concert. He was especially fond of a piece called "Platinum," but did not expect it would be played during the concert:

> The first notes made me almost pass out. It was Platinum! I felt that I disappeared for a moment and then woke up like in a dream but aware of the music all the time. Somehow I was soaring above the

audience that was merely there but could not be heard and did not disturb. It was like a dream, I was soaring and they played just for me. It is very hard to explain the feeling I had. That I was totally gone was observed by [my friends] E and A who had been trying to get in contact with me during the tune but failed. I regained my senses again when somebody hit my on my shoulder several times and shouted my name. That was E who wondered what was the matter. I was wet on my cheeks and had evidently been crying.

In the second, an American journalist recalls travelling on a bus in Morocco during Ramadan:

A young man got on with a boombox blasting a haunting and ululating Ramadan tune and, as the bus started again, held the box to his chin and sang in high, soulful tones, his gaze cast into the distance. I could not tell which words came from the box, and which from his mouth, and I was aware suddenly of how little I understood the spiritual tides surging round me. I was not in control; I was outside the frame.

In time, of course, I would come back within the frame, back to my familiar habits of observing and writing. But right then, on the bus, I was learning how rich it is to venture into that strange territory of the mind when you are bewildered and vulnerable - lost, even. I just listened to the music.

Both writers describe a loss of control: the first feels as though he is in a dream and soaring above the rest of the concert audience, while the second feels that he lacks control and is somehow "outside the frame." In both cases, the loss of control would seem to go beyond "everyday" experiences of listening to music.

EMOTIONALLY STRONG RESPONSES: POSITIVE OR NEGATIVE?

Are sublime or emotionally strong experiences of music positive or negative for those who undergo them? Listeners report both good and bad feelings arising from their strong experiences with music. Some, like our first writer who was impressed by Sibelius' *Second Symphony*, report feelings of *renewal, rejuvenation, liberation and purification* through music. The following two accounts, the first autobiographical, the second literary, illustrate these feelings:

> I was diving into the music [Beethoven's *Ninth Symphony*] and letting it surround me. I started singing along with the chorus. I got up from my seat and walked about my room. I felt exhilarated, released, joyous. I felt as if I were walking on air. My heart beat faster and I experienced a 'chill' in my spine.

In the next account, Proust's Swann compares a concert he attends with the memory of a performance he had heard the year before. At the earlier performance, the music had "opened and expanded" his soul:

> This time he had distinguished quite clearly a phrase which emerged for a few moments above the waves of sound. It had at once suggested to him a world of inexpressible delights, of whose existence, before hearing it, he had never dreamed, into which he felt that nothing else could initiate him; and he had been filled with love for it, as with a new and strange desire.
>
> With a slow and rhythmical movement it led him first this way, then that, towards a state of happiness that was noble, unintelligible, and yet precise.
>
> ... Indeed this passion for a phrase of music seemed, for a time, to open up before Swann the possibility of a sort of rejuvenation.

In both these accounts the listener's strong emotional experience of music is positive: feelings of joy, exhilaration, happiness, even rejuvenation.

We have already seen that such positive responses are not necessarily typical. In the two accounts of Tchaikovsky's *Pathétique*, the first listener reported intense physical pain and the second said that he felt "totally crushed" in certain passages. Remember also the American journalist's feelings of being lost and bewildered while listening to

Ramadan music on the bus in Morocco. Strong emotional responses to music may be negative as well as positive. Listeners have reported *anxiety, vulnerability, depletion,* even *horror.*

The following account illustrates the extent to which listening to music may be an uncomfortable experience. The writer recalls listening to a recording of Mahler's *10th Symphony* with his brother, one summer evening some days before the funeral of their beloved grandmother:

> The largest part of this symphony is heavenly Mahlerish stale stuff...But then, there it was. A chord so heart-rending and ghost-ridden that I had never experienced before. A single tone (a trumpet, if I remember it right) is added with an endless number of different instruments from the orchestra, not unlike a huge organ where you pull out every organ stop at random, a dissonance that pierced my very marrow. My brother and I reacted the same: we were both filled with such a primitive horror, almost prehistorical, that none of us could utter a single word. We both looked at the big black window and both of us seemed to see the face of death staring at us from outside. A face with a diameter of about two meters.
>
> It took me five years before I dared to listen to that piece again. The very thought of this chord gives me cold chills and a kind of atavistic horror, even today, fourteen years later.

It would seem, then, that sublime or emotionally strong emotional experiences of music may be pleasurable or painful for listeners. Before leaving this topic, I should mention that a listener may undergo both positive and negative emotions while listening to a single work. Consider the following:

> I was familiar with the particular piece of music [Ravel's *Bolero*] so there were many feelings of anxiety to hear the crescendos, great feelings of joy and laughter as the piece repeated itself to the final point. I applauded each time the violins interjected at their fierce pace. I was appreciative of the genius that made me feel so beautiful and refreshed inside.

Here, the writer reports negative feelings (anxiety) as well as positive (joy and rejuvenation). We should also note the physical responses (laughter) and feelings of social connections (appreciation for "the genius" - presumably the composer).

DIFFERENCES IN THE PERSONAL ACCOUNTS

So far we have mainly considered the ways in which descriptions of strong emotional responses to music are similar to one another. Of course, they may differ in various ways as well. The taste and musical preparation of a listener will influence whether he is moved by Bach, Beethoven or the Beatles. More significantly, listeners place *different cognitive or affective meaning and import* on their listening experiences, depending on personality, background, life situation and other factors. Surely the brothers who saw the face of death while listening to Mahler's 10th were influenced by the recent demise of their grandmother. Consider the following description by the philosopher Bryan Magee, of his mid-life crisis:

> I came to feel that the most characteristic distillation of the existentialist experience and sensibility was to be found not in the writings of any philosopher, nor in any plays or novels (as it might have been in those, say, of Jean-Paul Sartre) but in the symphonies of Mahler. These engaged with some of my own anxieties and insights with such force and precision that it was as if Mahler had buttonholed me personally. By the end of listening to one of them I would be wrung out, not *as if* I had been through an emotional experience that had drained me of all, but because I had. Indeed, not only had I been through such an experience, I had shared to the full in the existential depth of a personality, lived a life. Even the sometimes almost intolerable beautifulness of the music, demanding more of the listener than could be borne without distress, spoke directly of life and the world and experience as I knew them.

Magee's account shares features with some of the others we have read: negative feelings (of depletion or being "wrung out") and social connections with the composer. (Magee feels as though Mahler is addressing him personally and engaging with his own anxieties.) What is specific to Magee's account is the connection he makes with existential thought - surely a reflection of his engagement with philosophy.

The following account reflects a different life-history and orientation. It happened when the author was seven years old:

> I was sitting in morning assembly at school. The music formed part of the assembly service ... The music was a clarinet duet, classical, probably by Mozart. I was astounded at the beauty of the sound. It was liquid, resonant, vibrant. It seemed to send tingles through me. I felt as if it was a significant moment. Listening to this music led me to learning to play first the recorder and then to achieve my ambition of playing the clarinet ... Whenever I hear clarinets being played I remember the impact of this first experience.

The differences between these two experiences, Magee's and that of the listener above, are of course due in part to the different music each heard - Mahler in one case and Mozart in the other - and to the life-situation of each (middle-aged adult and a child). Yet they also reflect each listener's personality and background: Magee, a philosopher, readily hears philosophical themes in the music. The second author, a musician, finds the significance of the listening experience in its inspiring a career in music.

Cultural differences can also play a role in the experience of listening to music and in how listeners respond. Rousseau said of the tune "Ranz-des-Vaches":

> ... that Air so dear to the hearts of the Swiss that playing it in their Troops was forbidden on pain of death, because it made those who heard it weep, desert, or die, so ardent a desire did it arouse in them to see their country again.

The impact of the song is culturally specific, as Rousseau does not claim that anyone would be moved by "Ranz-des-Vaches." It has significance only for the Swiss. Another way in which cultural differences can influence the emotional experience of music is in the way that cultural expectations and norms guide the behaviour of the listeners. The following anecdote in taken from the tenth-century "Book of Songs" composed by Isfahani. The scene is a concert given by the famous singer Jamila at her home. She sings erotic verses by the poet 'Umar ibn-Abi Rabi'a, who is also present:

> As Jamila sang, all those gathered there were seized by *tarab* [ecstasy]: they began to clap their hands, beat time on the floor with their feet, and sway their heads, shouting: 'We offer ourselves in sacrifice for thee, oh Jamila, to protect you from all evil .... How sublime your song and your words!' As for the poet 'Umar, he began to shout out: 'Woe is me. Woe is me ...' He tore his robe from top to bottom, in a state of total unconsciousness. When he came to, he felt ashamed and began to apologize, saying: " 'By Allah, I could not restrain myself, for that beautiful voice made me lose my mind.' "

In Islam there is a tradition of strong emotional responses to music, both sacred music (as in the case of Dervishes) and secular, as above. Rending of garments and loss of consciousness are extreme responses, although not uncommonly reported. In the western tradition of emotional responses to music such behaviour is practically unknown. While emotional responses to music are personal, such responses nonetheless tend to take culturally approved forms.

SUMMING UP

In the emotionally strong response to music we have been reading about - experiences of the sublime - music is reported to cause changes in listeners' mental and emotional states. The listeners' affective response may (but need not) have physical manifestations, including muscular activity, changes in breathing and heart rates, tingles or chills, hair standing on end and changes in brain activity. Listeners may be aware of all of these physical changes, or they may not. The emotional charge of sublime experiences can be contrasted with both "unengaged" and "intellectual" responses to music. When listeners are unengaged and respond very little to music, it may be because the music is not of a high enough quality or sufficient novelty to hold their attention, or it may be because they are not suitably and sufficiently prepared to appreciate what the music has to offer. An intellectual response to music, on the other hand, is a type of voluntary listening strategy. The listener, perhaps by focusing on some particular aspect of the work or performance, resists becoming "lost" in the music and does not allow herself to be fully affected by it.

Sublime or emotionally strong responses can be arranged along a continuum, ranging from momentary chills or thrills to longer-duration, transcendent, even "out-of-body" experiences. They also may include feelings of deep yet quiet awe. Such experiences can be either intensely personal and private or boisterously social and communal. Sometimes music seems to be the dominant factor contributing to the experience (a single person in a darkened room listening to a recording) and sometimes music is one factor among several (many people participating in a ritual during which music is played). However, in the responses we have considered, feelings and thoughts aroused through listening are attributed by the listener to the music. Other features of the overall experience - for example, the time and place of the experience, the absence or presence of other listeners, the listeners' prior psychological states, their physical orientation or movements, and possible drug use - may also contribute. However, these "extra-musical" factors are not thought by the listener to be sufficient in themselves to produce the experience in question. If a listener thought that any of these other non-musical features was the sole or primary cause of her experience, we would hesitate to say that she had reported a strong or sublime experience *of music*.

Before we leave these descriptions I want to address any doubts that readers may have. All of the accounts in this chapter are retrospective self-reports. When social scientists ask people to reveal something about themselves - how many calories in a day they consume, whether or not they have been unfaithful to a spouse, how much money they spend on non-essential purchases - there is always a risk that the answers may not reflect the truth of the matter. It is not so much that people consciously set out to deceive researchers, although of course that may happen. Rather, people may misremember, or they may not actually have a clear idea about, say, how much food they consume in a day. While some of the descriptions we have considered recount recent events, some detail experiences which happened months if not years ago. How can we be sure that these listeners have not simply misremembered events, or embroidered them after the fact? Could these reports of pain and tears perhaps be exaggerated?

Of course, one cannot rule out memory lapses and exaggeration after the fact in any self-reports. Do these possibilities call into question whether music can *ever* cause strong emotional responses? There is such a consistency in the basic features of the accounts that differences in the details do not strike me as a problem. While autobiographical memories may not be literal representations, they may yet be accurate in representing the personal significance of an event. Indeed Gabrielsson and his team believe that such memories may be partly constructed to cohere with the individual's self-concept. It may be that some people like to think of themselves as particularly sensitive or vulnerable to music. So even if experiences of music are sometimes misremembered or exaggerated, the ways in which they are transformed in their re-telling is significant. If people remember music as affecting them more than it actually did, this says something about their relation to music and their conception of the power it has over them. I have stressed the similarities among various accounts, and the similarities to be found yet within various differences. Perhaps these similarities do not reflect similarities in experiences; rather, they may reflect similarities in the way we *discuss* our experiences. They may reflect a shared cultural vocabulary, rather than shared feelings and impressions. Again, this possibility cannot be ruled out, but it is not very troubling. If a common way of referring to and describing musical experience has evolved, then this tells us something about how we have come to understand the emotional experience of music.

But just because listeners conceive of music as having power does not show that it does in fact have this power. How can we be sure that the experiences of music described in this chapter really are experiences of *music*? Perhaps listeners are attributing to music a power to move them, all the while being influenced by different factors. After all, we have read of a midlife crisis, a dead grandmother, a bus trip in North Africa - who know what other factors listeners may have neglected to mention?

There is no simple way to quell this worry. The listener may indeed be deluded; so may the researcher. A listener's immediate surroundings and life history certainly play a role in how she experiences music. Listening to music never occurs in a vacuum; the immediate context is nearly always relevant. Later, I will argue that listening to music - even solitary listening - is best thought of as a social phenomenon. Attempts to "filter out" and set aside extraneous influences and focus on the effect of the music "itself" are suspect if we want to understand the whole story of how listeners respond to music in real-life situations. Nonetheless, in each of the descriptions we have considered, listeners attribute their feelings and reactions to music, not to other factors (although they may recognize that these play a role). Indeed, the presence of music is a common denominator that cuts across the various accounts and the glimpses of different personalities. And again, even if listeners are mistaken, this says something about the way we think about music and about its power over us. Each listener may be mistaken; the thought that all are deluded in a systematic way cannot be ruled out. Yet it seems forced and invidious to claim that the questioner alone sees through it all.

Given the inherent limitations of self-reports it is a good idea, whenever possible, to supplement them with different kinds of investigations - ones that are not as vulnerable to the tricks of memory or wishful thinking. We do this in later chapters.

* * *

We have heard listeners speak for themselves and recount their own strong emotional responses to music. They described a wide variety of listening situations and mentioned many different musical works. Is any one kind of music more likely than another to provoke a strong response? Or are such responses inspired by specific sonic features, which may be found in any type of music? Are great works more likely to move listeners? In the next chapter we move from considering listeners to contemplating music in an attempt to answer these questions.

4

THE MUSIC ITSELF

ONE OF THE STRIKING FEATURES OF THE PERSONAL
ACCOUNTS in chapter 3 is the very wide variety of musical works that
were said to arouse strong emotional responses. Works mentioned included
classical or art music, pop and non-western music; symphonic works
and solo compositions; and pieces from the baroque era, the Romantic
period and the twentieth century. In the full set of reports collected by
the SEM Project there is music from seemingly every genre and from
a number of folk traditions. A survey of musical experts (participants
at the sixth meeting of the International Society for Music Perception
and Cognition) also found that a wide variety of music could arouse
emotional responses. Those attending the meeting were asked about the
last time they had been affected by a piece of music; researchers found
that emotional reactions were elicited by both classical and non-classical
music of various kinds, including the music of a big band concert given
the previous evening at the conference. While the wide variety of music
mentioned in these various surveys and personal accounts is striking,
so too is the recurrence of specific works. This is even more noticeable
when you examine a large number of personal accounts. Tchaikovsky's
Pathétique is cited again and again, as are the symphonies of Mahler
and Beethoven. Later, we shall see that Albinoni's Adagio, sections of
Bach's *St. Matthew Passion*, Mozart's "Tuba Mirum" from his *Requiem* and
Whitney Houston's rendition of the song "I Will Always Love You" have
been shown to be capable of provoking strong responses in listeners. Do

these musical works share anything, besides the fact that some people somewhere find them affecting? Are there specific features of music *qua* music which seem to be particularly affecting? Can we make any general claims about the music which arouses strong emotional responses?

A number of empirical psychological studies have tried to find out more about the music which is reported to provoke strong emotional responses, but these studies should be interpreted with caution. We shall have to be content with suggestions and indications; the quest for absolute certainty or "proof" would be misplaced here. There are a number of reasons for this circumspection. Most obviously, the small number of studies and the differences among their results limit the generality of the conclusions. Second, researchers tend to be interested in a more or less limited range of phenomena, and this interest guides their investigations. We have a few studies on specific physical responses (chills, tears or a combination thereof), and a sizeable anthropological literature on trance states in various cultures. Finally, the entire question of emotional responses to music is controversial and still not well understood. The editors of a recent definitive collection of essays on music and emotion state that no psychologist has attempted to write a monograph on the topic because it is too difficult to present a coherent story based on the available literature.

MUSIC AND TRANCE STATES

Trance states are a good place to start, as they are among the most extreme possible responses to music. In the popular imagination, and according to some researchers, trance states are associated with rhythmic drumming. This was not always the case. Plato associated trance states not with any specific rhythm, but with melodies played on the aulos, a wind instrument with a reed, probably like an oboe, but usually translated as "flute" or "pipes," as in Alcibiades' speech by in praise of Socrates in the *Symposium*:

> And you're quite a flute-player, aren't you? In fact you're much more marvellous than Marsyas, who needed instruments to cast his spells on people. And so does anyone who plays his tunes today - for even the tunes Olympos played are Marsyas' work,

since Olympos learned everything from him. Whether they are played by the greatest flautist or the meanest flute-girl, his melodies have in themselves the power to possess and so reveal those people who are ready for the god and his mysteries. That's because his melodies are themselves divine. (215c-d)

The view that the melody of an aulos is (at least partially) responsible for the onset of a trance state was shared by Aristotle and the ancient Greek playwrights Aeschylus, Sophocles and Euripides. Aristotle makes a more specific association between trance states and a certain tonal pattern - the Phrygian mode, which by its very nature is supposed to arouse the wild excitement associated with the frenzied celebration of ecstatic religions. As he writes in the *Politics*:

Yet among the modes the Phrygian has exactly the same effect as the pipes [*aulos*] among instruments: both are orgiastic and emotional, for all Bacchic frenzy and all similar agitation are associated with the pipes more than with other instruments, and such conduct finds its appropriate expression in the tunes composed in the Phrygian mode more than in those composed in other modes. (1342a)

More recently, the ethnomusicologist Gilbert Rouget has written a masterful and comprehensive study on the relations between music and possession trances, examining a great number of cultures from around the world. He has found that the connections between music and trance may vary a great deal, depending on the cult in question, the stage reached by the adept, the state of the adept at the particular time and the ritual in question. Music may play a decisive role in inducing a trance, or (rarely) it may play no role. As a general rule a possession fit or trance is accompanied by music, and music is almost always regarded as being more or less responsible for its onset. Examining the music used in possession rituals throughout the world, Rouget finds as many different kinds of possession music as there are cults. Yet he discerns two recurring features in such music: breaks or abrupt changes in rhythm; and passages where the music simultaneously accelerates and grows louder.

Reading Rouget's descriptions of trance-inducing music aroused my curiosity and I decided to seek out such music for myself. The next time I was in the "world" section of a large music store I purchased a documentary recording entitled "Witchcraft and Ritual Music," recorded in Kenya and Tanzania (Nonesuch Explorer Series 79708-2). I listened to the whole CD a couple of times, and then concentrated on two tracks which seem to be the clearest examples of the kind of music described by Rouget. The first was from the Bantu-speaking Taita tribe. The liner notes explain: "Witch doctors of the Taita prescribe the healing power of drums to help sick women relinquish control of their movements. After the patients have been possessed by the spirit of the drums for several hours, sometimes for days, their illnesses are expelled from their bodies." The second selection, "Giriama Spirit Dance," from a different tribe, was similarly associated with the healing of a sick woman possessed by spirits. The first selection is nearly five minutes long and the second just over two minutes, but both give the impression that the recording begins *in media res*. Drum rhythms dominate both, but I could also hear other percussion (including handclaps?) and human voices. I could easily recognize the point (as described by Rouget) when the music becomes both louder and faster at the same time. The music is interesting, even absorbing; but in the end it was too exotic and strange to me to make much of a genuine impression. I simply did not have the relevant musical and cultural background that would have made the music "speak" to me; I remained a tourist. It hardly needs to be said that I did not fall into a trance.

TEARS AND CHILLS - STRUCTURAL ASPECTS OF MUSIC

While trance states are a feature of the religious practices of many different cultures all over the world, they are not something most of us encounter on a daily basis. Much more common are various strongly marked but less intense responses to music: moist eyes, tearing up and chills down the spine. Although tears and chills (also known as shivers, goose bumps, frissons and tingles) are distinct responses, it makes sense to examine them together. When tears and chills occur in close association it might be difficult to distinguish the causes of one from the causes of the other. A further complication is that experimental conditions might discourage some from "letting loose" and weeping in response to music; whereas chills, being less noticeable, may not be similarly inhibited. Hence treating tears and chills separately might turn out to be misleading in the end.

One finding comes up repeatedly in empirical studies of emotional responses to music: music that is familiar to the listener is more likely than unfamiliar music to elicit strong responses. This is not to say that any familiar music was more effective in eliciting a response than any unfamiliar music; just that people tended to experience strong responses more routinely to familiar music, or to music they themselves had selected, than to unfamiliar music. This would seem to indicate two things. The first is the importance of personal associations in strong emotional responses to music. We tend to feel more strongly about music that we already have some connection to, and familiar music may also accompany personal memories. Second, long acquaintance with a musical work is no obstacle to responding to it with deep emotion. The old saying that "familiarity breeds contempt" seems not to hold true when it comes to music!

Some of the first studies on music-related tears and chills were carried out by the music psychologist John Sloboda and published in 1991. Sloboda asked British adults to complete a questionnaire in their own time on their physical responses to music in the past five years. He also asked them to identify the musical event associated with the response, be it a phrase, motif or chord, and, if possible, to make reference to the event in the work's score. Those who completed the survey reported physical sensations such as chills, tears, lumps in the throat and racing hearts, among others. Sloboda then looked at the musical selections his informants claimed were most likely to prompt tears, and found that they were associated with three musical features in particular. Tears were most reliably provoked by melodic appogiaturas, and to a lesser extent by melodic or harmonic sequences, and by harmonic movements through the cycle of fifths to the tonic. An "appogiatura" (often notated with a grace note) is a dissonant note preceding a note in a melody and taking up part of its time value. A melodic or harmonic sequence is the repetition of a melodic or harmonic pattern at a different pitch. Several of the works which Sloboda found to elicit tears shared all three of these structural features. Examples include the opening of Albinoni's Adagio, the opening chorus of Bach's *St. Matthew Passion*, Musetta's song from Puccini's opera *La Bohème*, the opening of the third movement of Rachmaninov's *Second Symphony*, and the "love theme" from Tchaikovsky's *Romeo and Juliet*. Sloboda found a somewhat different set of musical structural features in the passages which were thought to provoke chills. New or unprepared harmonies and sudden dynamic or textural change, often occurring together, were most often associated with chills, and second most often with (once again) melodic appogiaturas. Beethoven's *Fourth Piano Concerto*, a work which many of the respondents claimed gave them chills, has at least three instances in the first movement where new or unprepared harmonies occur together with dynamic or textural change.

Sloboda's article inspired more work on emotional responses to music, in particular on the chill response, and these later findings have been largely in line with what Sloboda discovered in his research. One such study was a 1995 paper by the neuroscientist and psychobiologist Jaak Panksepp based on years of research with American college students. Panksepp limited his investigations to one physical phenomenon - chills - and most of the musical selections he used in his experiments were popular songs. Although he worked with different musical genres, a different experimental method and a different population (American college students rather than British adults) his results were similar to those found by Sloboda. Again, dramatic crescendos were associated with chills. One song in particular, Pink Floyd's "Post War Dream," was seen to be extremely effective in provoking chills. A time-series analysis indicated that the majority of chills occurred in response to an intense crescendo at the beginning of the second minute.

The most recent research that I know of on musical chills was carried out at the University of Geneva. Researchers asked 243 students to rate thirty classical music excerpts, each two minutes long, according to a wide range of descriptive terms. Out of these thirty excerpts, the six that were most often given a "chill" label became the subject of further tests. A different, smaller selection of student volunteers who described themselves as physically susceptible to music were then asked to listen to the six excerpts and press a button when they felt a chill coming on. The top three "chill-inducing" excerpts were, in order: The opening measures of Mozart's *Piano Concerto* No. 23 K488, second movement; the first twenty-five measures of Bruch's *Kol Nidrei*; and the opening of Chopin's *First Piano Concerto*, second movement. The particular passages associated with a chill responses in each of these works shared several similarities. All were slow and characterized by a crescendo or rise in volume from *piano* (soft) to *forte* (loud). Each featured an alternation between the solo instrument and the orchestra. Finally, each of the passages was built around an unexpected harmonic progression.

The authors of the Geneva study suggest that the combination of formal features they found in their top three excerpts elicited a feeling of "ambiguity" in listeners. Their remark is a potent reminder that, in the hands of a great composer, the structural features of a musical work are never merely the organization of interrelated parts. They are expressive tools and communicate something to listeners, however hard it is to say exactly what that something might be. If our discussion of music remains technical, we can lose sight of the way listeners experience musical works. Take, for example, Bruch's *Kol Nidrei*, a piece I have loved since childhood when I used to listen to a scratchy LP of it performed by the great and supremely expressive cellist Pablo Casals. The formal description of the opening phrases as slow, characterized by a crescendo and built around an unexpected harmonic passage does nothing to convey its emotional power and intensity. When performed by a skilled and sensitive musician, the resignation and sadness conveyed in the music are extremely poignant, even heartrending. We need not accept, as it has been argued in the past, that non-technical discussions of music reflect impoverished understanding. Both ways of talking about music are required and each has its own advantages. It may be a more straightforward matter to decide whether a harmony is unprepared than to decide whether a specific work really is melancholy. What non-technical language lacks in precision and clarity it can make up for in its descriptive power. For instance, many musical works of a very different character share the feature of a harmonic movement through the cycle of fifths to the tonic. A technical description may then be of little help in conveying how the particular piece we are interested in would be heard and described by listeners. Less technical language can capture how (more or less) naïve listeners describe music and the qualities of music they tend to find moving.

Like the Geneva researchers, Panksepp also stresses the expressive and emotive qualities of the music he uses in his research. He notes that for chills to occur with any consistency, a certain type of expressive background may also be important. Chills seem to be most readily provoked by moods of bitter-sweetness, melancholy and sadness. He sees one of his most significant findings as the association of chills with sad rather than happy music. The results of one of his studies indicate that the descriptions of the two emotions with the highest relationship to the number of chills were "sad/melancholy" and "thoughtful/nostalgic." The other emotional qualities tested - "happy/excited," "reverent/peaceful," "fearful/anxious," "anger/hate," "patriotic/triumphant" and "passionate/sexuality" - were not found to have any positive relationship to chills. Indeed, Panksepp doubts whether any thoroughly happy music that is unfamiliar to the listener would provoke a chill response. Chills that seem to be provoked during happy music are more likely to be caused by those sections of the music where happiness and sadness are thoroughly entangled and hence bittersweet. Therefore, a musical work's expressive shape over its course - the succession of more or less intensely happy and sad passages - may be important to the chill experience. Jerrold Levinson, a philosopher whose work offers a sustained and illuminating discussion of the various pleasures of art and music, has argued that the crucial determinant of the chill experience is music's poignancy of expression (or expression of poignancy). He writes that life itself has a mixed character, with happiness and sadness, good things and bad, inextricably intertwined. Some of the music that moves us most deeply reflects this quality. Hence musical works that do not speak to anything "profound" in human nature, though they may be enjoyable and well structured, will be unlikely to induce the chill experience. In support of the "bittersweet" or poignancy hypothesis, we may note that the entry on "Tears" in the nineteenth-century *Grand Larousse* encyclopedia reported that a "trivial little piece" called "Joy Causes Fear" prompted the shedding, every evening for nearly a year, "of the most aristocratic of tears."

Just as an unexpected harmonic progression can have expressive value, so too can crescendos. They are more than just increases in volume and also contribute to a musical work's emotional intensity. Indeed, this is how Panksepp interprets the crescendos in Pink Floyd's "Post-War Dream" and in other chill-inducing works. He believes that such peaks are an "optimal stimulus" for the generation of chills. Similarly, emotional intensity can be conveyed through "the piercing simplicity of certain solo pieces that emerge from a richer orchestral background." Panksepp has found that certain types of sustained high-frequency notes, again often presented by a solo performer such as a soprano voice, violin or cello and executed with an unrelenting and piercing quality, is ideal for generating chills. Panksepp cautions that this hypothesis has not yet been empirically tested, but he offers some anecdotal support. For several years he has held informal competitions in his classes to see which recent popular song produces the most chills. In 1994 he found that Whitney Houston's "I Will Always Love You" to be "far and away" the most effective stimulus for producing chills among his students. Interestingly, the writer John Seabrook invokes the same song to illustrate the emotional climax that popular music business professionals sometimes call the "money note." This is "that moment on the record which seems to have an almost involuntary effect on your insides. ... The money note is the moment in Whitney Houston's version of the Dolly Parton song 'I Will Always Love You' at the beginning of the third rendition of the chorus: pause, drum beat, and then 'Iiiiiieeeeeeiiieeii will always love you.'"

Panksepp and Seabrook are not the only ones who believe that the sound of a soprano voice is particularly conducive to experiences of the sublime in music. The French psychoanalyst Michel Poizat examined the experience of *jouissance* (elation, ecstasy or gratification, manifested in tears and chills) among opera lovers in Paris. His general thesis is that listeners start to weep at the moment when language disappears and meaning dissolves, only to be gradually superseded by a cry that escapes the logic of verbal expression. We can hear this happening when the voice (especially a soprano) seems to extend beyond itself, reaching for very high pitches, putting the words sung under great tension. Listeners start to cry when a single tone is held for what seems to be an impossibly long time; then there is a break just before the end as the singer silently gasps for breath. Poizat conjectures that listeners somehow sense that the voice they hear has almost broken free of language; yet at the same time they know that the voice can never break free of language.

Do the musical works which have been reported to cause chills in listeners have anything in common other than certain formal features and a certain bitter-sweet or poignant expressive character? Levinson proposes an additional quality of music conducive to the chill experience: fineness of expression, whether understood as depth, intensity or exquisiteness. Such "fineness" could presumably be found in musical works themselves or in exemplary performances of them. For the first time in our discussion considerations of beauty or aesthetic value emerge, as "fineness," "depth," "intensity" and "exquisiteness" are all positively value-laden terms. Is it only great musical works or masterpieces that arouse tears and chills in listeners? Can we even say with confidence which musical works deserve to be called "great"? These questions will occupy us later.

LISTENING TO MUSIC

No description of music, however technically precise or valuable as literature in its own right, can take the place of hearing the music for oneself. I hope that readers not already familiar with some of the works discussed so far will be intrigued enough to seek them out and listen for themselves. When I first read about the music that inspired strong responses in Sloboda's initial research, I was motivated to think about music that I had found moving in the past. In fall 2000, while a visiting professor at Lewis and Clark College in Portland, Oregon, I met the composer Forrest Pierce, who kindly agreed to visit my senior seminar in the philosophy of music. Forrest discussed with us how composers create musical meaning through a variety of techniques. One of his central examples was Chopin's *Prelude No. 20 in C minor*, opus 28, which he played on the piano. I recall being very struck by the piece, and remembered it long after I had forgotten his other musical examples. So much has happened since then that "being struck" is about all I can recall of my initial emotional response. Shortly thereafter I happened to be given one of those boxed CD sets of popular classical music and was happy to find that it contained a number of Chopin preludes, including the one in C minor performed by Russell Sherman. When I listen to the prelude now, I am struck again by its power and seeming simplicity. Every tone seems pregnant. It follows a basic ABB structure; each segment is four bars long and the piece ends with a C minor chord. The dynamic marking for section A is "ff" (very loud); "p" (soft) for section B; and "pp" (very soft) for the repeat of section B. There is a crescendo marking two bars before the final chord. The overall emotional colour of the piece is sombre, yet somehow also poignant, even profound. If pressed, I would say that the prelude expresses something like resignation to fate, mingled with a faint glimmer of hope. The final few bars, though, suggest increasing confidence, and the concluding tonic chord expresses, perhaps, acceptance.

I wondered if this prelude shares any of the musical-structural features that Sloboda and other researchers have found in the works associated with strong emotional responses. There are no dramatic crescendos, no unprepared harmonies or appogiaturas. The work abounds with melodic and harmonic sequences, although the harmonic movement is not through the cycle of fifths. While all of this is interesting and made me feel as though I had a better grasp of the piece than before, none of it helped me come any closer to identifying what it is about the prelude that I find so moving. Why should I find it profound? As a teacher of philosophy I cannot help but feel faintly embarrassed at doing so; philosophers tend to be parsimonious with the term and careful about what they apply it to. This feeling is compounded when a colleague tells me that Chopin's C minor is the famous "Barry Manilow" prelude - the tune is the basis for his song "Could it be Magic?" written with Adrienne Anderson, and whose lyrics are anything but profound.

The Chopin prelude is poignant, and the "expressive narrative" I found in it (sombre resignation-hope-increasing confidence) fits

Levinson's description of the music he thought most likely to bring about chills in listeners. With this suggestion in mind, I continued to listen to some of the music found to provoke strong emotional responses in others. Albinoni's Adagio, another very popular work, has been recorded many times, transcribed for a variety of instruments and featured on the soundtracks of several films. A friend who is a professional violinist and who makes extra money by playing in small ensembles at weddings, tells me that it is by far the most frequently requested piece. The version I listened to is a transcription for organ and orchestra, performed by the Toronto Symphony Orchestra under the direction of Sir Andrew Davis. Their performance is not as slow as some I have heard; things keep flowing and moving along. The piece sounds yearning, but also restful, luminous, beautiful. It is not hard to understand its popularity. While the music is very expressive it is difficult to say precisely what it expresses. I am unable to find a definite "expressive narrative"; the music does not seem to point to anything outside itself. I can imagine several narrative constructions that might be appropriate, but nothing in particular springs to mind. Settling on a single narrative would seem to burden the work unfairly with my own expectations and preconceptions.

What about the specific musical works mentioned in the empirical studies? Panksepp published his research on Pink Floyd's "Post War Dream" in 1995, and it did not surprise me to read that the song was unfamiliar to nearly two-thirds of his students. When I was a high school student in Canada in the early 1980s, the English rock band was already considered somewhat of a *recherché* taste. Of Panksepp's subjects who did recognize the song, I wonder how many would have had the same associations with the band as I did - "intellectual," quirky art rock that was somehow just outside the mainstream, despite the huge number of albums they sold.

Eager to test my memories against Panksepp's research, I borrowed their CD *The Final Cut* from the local library. "Post War Dream" was the first track, and I soon realized that I had heard it before yet never learned the title. It begins with the sound of a radio dial being turned and the voices of several British announcers. Slowly and softly, a rich texture of orchestral sound behind the voices grows louder as the voices fade. The orchestra plays a simple, slow, "church-like" melody as the voice of the lead singer begins:

> Tell me true, tell me why
> Was Jesus crucified?
> Was it for this that Daddy died?
> Was it you, was it me
> Did I watch too much TV?
> Is that a hint of accusation in your eye?

As the "dramatic crescendo" builds, the voice of the lead singer and the orchestra are joined by rock instruments, with the latter eventually taking over. While I did not experience chills, I could recognize that the song is clearly well put together and effective in drawing me in, especially the first few times I listened. I am not surprised that college students who had never heard it before (and hear it only once or twice) might be impressed and even moved. Yet on repeated listening, the combined banality and pretension of the lyrics become irritating. Earnest appeals to Margaret Thatcher ("Maggie, what have we done?") now sound dated, even quaint. I can understand why rock critics damned the album as "another long whine from a rich, jaded rock star."

While many of Panksepp's students had not previously heard "Post War Dream," I feel almost sure that they would have been familiar with Whitney Houston's "I Will Always Love You." Indeed, can there be anyone in the developed world who has not heard it? Recorded in 1992 for the soundtrack of the film *The Bodyguard*, it was a huge hit and seemed to be on the radio constantly for several years afterward. Wanting to compare my response with that of the students, I purchased and downloaded the song from iTunes, and then really listened to it, as opposed to overhearing it while occupied by something else. The song begins with Houston's unaccompanied voice singing softly, with a great deal of *rubato* (rhythmic freedom rather than adherence to a strict tempo). As she begins the first chorus, her voice is joined by stringed instruments and an electric guitar. With the second verse the tempo becomes more regular (drum beats join the other instruments), and

Houston's voice grows louder. I am struck by how her very expressive and emotional performance belies the song's lyrics, which recycle pop-song platitudes of the "I'm leaving but it's not your fault, and I still love you" variety. (She sounds so much in love! Can she really be leaving for good?) After the second chorus there is a soaring saxophone solo, then the pause, drum beat and third chorus described by Seabrook. The song is surprisingly effective when one surrenders to it, even if this kind of overblown pop music is not a preferred taste. Houston's voice is undeniably powerful and every detail of the production - the unaccompanied beginning, the slow and gradual crescendo and deepening of musical texture, the sax solo - seems to add to the expressive impact. I did not experience chills as I listened, but I admit that the song gets under my skin, despite myself. I feel the way I sometimes do when I tear up at a Hollywood movie: fully aware that the film-makers are manipulating the audience and that I should not be emotional over a silly movie. But tears come on regardless.

Somewhat later I discussed Houston's rendition of "I Will Always Love You" with a colleague who is extremely knowledgeable about popular music. He told me how much he preferred Dolly Parton's original version for its simple and dignified yet moving take on the song. People who care about music a great deal often stress the virtues of particular performances. A certain performer or conductor might be able to bring out aspects of the work that others do not, or even to revitalize a familiar warhorse. So when I decided to listen carefully to Tchaikovsky's *Pathétique Symphony*, I consulted with musically savvy friends and with the salesman at "Sam the Record Man" to find the most lush, emotional performance I could and decided on a recent, critically acclaimed recording by the St Petersburg Philharmonic, conducted by Yuri Temirkanov. The very quiet beginning with its soft, low tones drew me in. The work's dynamic range is such that when I listened to the symphony on my iPod I found myself adjusting the volume frequently, even within a single movement. Together with the dynamic range goes a great deal of emotional variability; it is not called the "pathetic" or "emotional" symphony for nothing. I was reminded of the mercurial heroines of Russian literature, and I was not surprised that some listeners reported feeling drained by the symphony. As with the Albinoni, the symphony did not suggest to me a single specific expressive narrative, although I can imagine several that might fit.

Perhaps more than any other canonical work, the Pathétique polarizes critical opinion. I recall hearing an announcer on the radio once say that he disdained the symphony because one of its major themes (beginning roughly near the end of the fourth minute) was used as the basis for a cheesy popular song ("Full moon and empty arms ..."). I can certainly sympathize; the slow movement of Rachmaninov's Second Symphony has been ruined for me because its melody forms the basis of a different but equally awful popular song. Yet it is worth remembering that in neither case is this the composer's fault. The philosopher Colin Radford went so far as to argue that Tchaikovsky's symphony is immoral. According to him, the symphony expresses and can induce or reinforce in listeners the feeling of sentimentality, an outlook Radford finds morally unworthy. Robert Sharpe, another philosopher who has discussed the symphony and the range of opinion on it, also does not hide his disregard for the work. Yet others, whose musical taste and judgement I greatly respect, consider it a masterwork. The *Pathétique* is enormously popular; might some of its detractors be motivated by snobbery? ("Can it really be any good, if so many people like it?" I can almost hear them asking.) Of course, the source of their motivation has nothing to do with the truth or falsity of their judgements. I suspect that legitimate differences of taste play an important role here. Emotional volatility is not everyone's cup of tea; it can be entertaining to read about those flighty and inconstant heroines, but one would not necessarily choose them as room-mates.

SUMMING UP

It seems clear that specific structural and sonic features of music are often associated with strong emotional responses. But we do not yet have in place the elements for an answer to the question of why music moves us. The structural and sonic features of music we have uncovered do not supply us with anything like necessary or sufficient conditions for strong responses. That is, there seems to be no feature of music without which a strong emotional response is impossible, and no feature which always prompts a strong response in listeners. The features of music we have discussed - appogiaturas, dramatic crescendos, unprepared harmonies, melodic and harmonic sequences, piercing tones emerging from a minimal background - occur in many different musical works. Only a limited number of these works have been associated in certain listeners with strong emotional responses. Similarly, certain expressive qualities in music, specifically the mixture of positive and negative emotion, have been associated with strong emotional responses. This kind of bitter-sweet or poignant quality occurs particularly frequently in music from the Romantic period. Again, such expressive qualities are not to be found in all of the works which arouse strong emotional responses. We can speak with greater confidence when it comes to the artistic quality of the works that prompt strong emotional responses. Idiosyncrasies and personal associations aside, many of the works which people find move them the most are also among the greatest musical works in their respective genres. The reason why this should be so is not hard to understand. Becoming involved with a musical work deeply enough to be moved by it requires that the work be of sufficient quality to hold one's attention and interest. Music that cannot hold the attention of a suitably educated and prepared listener will be unlikely to arouse a strong positive response.

If strong responses to music cannot be fully explained by features of music itself, how might they be explained? This is the question we undertake in the next chapter.

5

EXPLAINING STRONG EMOTIONAL RESPONSES TO MUSIC I

REDUCTIVE EXPLANATIONS

THE MUSICIAN FRANK ZAPPA recalls that when he was in high school, he took one of his favourite R&B songs to his band teacher, hoping that the teacher could help him understand why he liked it so much. The teacher listened to the song and replied, "parallel fourths," thereby explaining the song's appeal entirely by virtue of a single tonal pattern. Zappa's teacher said nothing about the song's lyrics, its emotional qualities, its rhythmic patterns, the beauty or inventiveness of its melody, the particular qualities of the singers' and instrumentalists' performance or the song's artistic merit. He also said nothing about Zappa's likely state of mind when listening to the song, or about the possible personal associations that Zappa might have already made with it. Zappa's teacher offered a reductive explanation; indeed, a less satisfying reductive explanation would be difficult to invent! A reductive explanation makes sense of a sophisticated or complex phenomenon by claiming that it is "nothing but" something simpler.

It is easy to see that the explanation offered by Zappa's teacher was not satisfying. If all there was to writing a great song was the inclusion of parallel fourths, then there would be many more great songs than there are. Yet reductive explanations are not necessarily inadequate just because they are reductive. Sometimes complex phenomena can indeed be fully explained in virtue of something less complex. Two different kinds of reductive strategies are sometimes employed in explaining strong emotional responses to music. First, the aural or sonic qualities of the music are seen to cause the responses. One researcher has called this the "pharmaceutical model" of musical understanding and he claims that it still dominates much psychological theorizing and experimentation. According to this model listeners are largely passive; music is a physical stimulus that mechanically affects their brains and bodies much as a drug would. A second kind of reductive strategy construes sublime responses to music as reflecting the psychology of affected listeners. It is thought that certain kinds of listeners will be more likely than others to have such responses. While neither of these strategies is ultimately appealing in itself, attention to the reasons provided for each can help us come, eventually, to a more satisfactory explanation.

A good example of the first kind of reductive strategy is found in the work of Andrew Neher on trance states. In the 1920s and 1930s Hans Berger had changed the field of neuroscience when he discovered what came to be known as the brain's alpha rhythm. This is a rhythmic oscillation with a frequency of about ten per second that occurs when subjects are relaxed and unoccupied with their eyes closed; the rhythm can be detected by electrodes applied to the head. Opening the eyes or performing a mental task such as solving a maths problem makes the rhythm disappear. The British researchers E. D. Adrian and B. H. C. Matthews in 1934 found that the alpha rhythm could be built up in amplitude and made to assume the frequency of a flashing light. Inspired by their research, Neher investigated the effect of rhythmic drumming on brain rhythms. He found that brain rhythms were indeed affected, especially in the regions associated with auditory perception. Neher also found muscle twitching in some subjects, and that others reported "unusual" perceptions. He wondered about the connections between these findings and the phenomenon of "unusual behaviour" (hallucinations and trance states) in ceremonies involving drums. When Neher examined ethnographic reports of behaviour observed in such ceremonies, he concluded that the behaviour was primarily the result of rhythmic drumming on the central nervous system.

There are a number of problems with Neher's proposal that trance states are caused by rhythmic drumming. First, a wide variety of instruments is associated with trance states. You may recall that in ancient Greece it was the music of the aulos, not the drums, that was thought to cause trance states. The acoustic signals known to accompany trance states are too radically different to have the same physiological effects on listeners. Second, in Africa very intense drum music is used in several contexts, including feasts and weddings, which are not associated with trance states. Indeed, with the significant exception of initiation trances and ceremonies, the music associated with trance states is of a piece with the group's everyday and popular music. Similarly, the aulos was played at many different occasions in ancient Greece, including symposia, where there is no record of a trance ever taking place. Third, even where drum rhythms are associated with trance states, not everyone present is affected; for instance, performing musicians do not usually fall into trance states. With the state of our current knowledge, there is no valid theory to justify the idea that the triggering of a trance can be attributed to the neurophysiological effects of drum sounds; indeed, there is at present no clear causal explanation for the induction of trance states. The ethnomusicologist Gilbert Rouget notes that if Neher's explanation were correct, "half of Africa would be in a trance from the beginning of the year to the end." Where drum rhythms are important in inducing trance states, they must be so for different kinds of reasons.

Researchers in the US recently investigated the connection between drumming and trance states. The results of the experiment should be worrying for anyone who wants to insist on a clear causal relationship between the two. In one experiment, participants were divided into two groups and asked to sit calmly with their eyes closed in a dimly lit room. One group listened to a recording of a live drummer beating out a steady rhythm for fifteen minutes; the other group sat in silence for the same length of time. At the end of the session, participants filled out a questionnaire and were invited to write comments in their own words about the experience. When asked about their experiences, the two groups did not differ from each other significantly in terms of positive emotional feelings, visual imagery, self-awareness or internal dialogue. So while monotonous drumming may influence subjects' brainwaves, it does not necessarily follow that differences in brainwave patterns must always be noticed by subjects or have any effect on them.

Moving from trance states to more common responses to music, Panksepp offers a more promising, yet still reductive, explanation for the origin of the chill phenomenon. He argues that chills may emerge from brain dynamics associated with the perception of social loss, specifically with separation calls. Separation calls are cries by young animals that inform parents of the whereabouts of offspring that have become lost. Typically, these calls arouse care-giving responses in parents. The "coldness" of chills may provide increased motivation for social reunion in the parents. Panksepp suggests that the chill we feel especially intensely during sad and bitter-sweet songs "occurs because that type of music resonates with the ancient emotional circuits that establish internal social values. Sad music may achieve its beauty and its chilling effect by juxtaposing a symbolic rendition of the separation call (a high-pitched crescendo or a solo instrument emerging from the background) in the emotional context of potential reunion and redemption." Panksepp is convinced that this hypothesis explains much of the data uncovered in his studies of the chill phenomenon in response to music.

Panksepp's evolutionary hypothesis, if it is correct, helps us understand why certain kinds of leaps in pitch and high-pitch voices and instruments may be moving. Certainly, parents who could respond quickly and effectively to their offspring's separation calls would be more likely to ensure the latter's survival and their own genetic continuation. We shall see later that the expressive qualities of music and its status as a social phenomenon will be important when we try to account for strong emotional responses to music, more broadly construed. In the meantime we should note a worry about Panksepp's hypothesis: even if it is plausible, it helps us understand only a limited range of the chill phenomenon (not all of the music which prompts chills is reminiscent of separation calls), and a limited range of strong emotional responses to music more generally.

The pharmaceutical or "stimulation" model of musical understanding and appreciation has its first modern expression in the philosopher René Descartes' early and often overlooked work *The Compendium of Music*, from around 1618. Descartes does not seem to have had much interest in music and even confessed in a letter that he could not distinguish between a fifth and an octave! The fact that he nonetheless wrote about music testifies to its importance as an area of intellectual inquiry at the time. According to Descartes, we are "naturally impelled" by music to move our bodies. Music affects our "animal spirits," which are roused to motion by certain rhythms. Despite their name, the animal spirits were physical in nature. Descartes conceived of them as liquids that moved through the nerves (which were thought to be small tubes) and allowed us to move our muscles at will. This stimulation of our animal spirits by music has two results. First, pleasure is aroused when the animal spirits are set in motion. Second, music arouses emotions by stimulating the animal spirits, and this arousal is itself pleasurable. The philosopher Peter Kivy has pointed out the inadequacies in Descartes' account, and he is convinced that these same shortcomings recur in the work of later thinkers. The problems with the pharmaceutical model lie in its conception of the musical object as a mere stimulus, rather than as a cognitive object. Kivy points out that if music were a mere stimulus, a listener's level of musical knowledge would have no effect on her pleasure in listening to music. Yet an educated listener is not like a pharmacologist who gets no more pleasure from heroin because he knows all about its molecular structure. Rather, knowledge about music, such as the awareness that certain things are going on technically, and knowledge of the difficulties involved in producing certain sounds on different instruments, makes for a more complex perceptual object. Knowledge about music gives you more to think about and this in turn can increase your appreciation of music and the pleasure you derive from listening to it. Even for the most naïve listener, music is not a mere physical stimulus but a perceived and cognized object, understood under one description or another.

Fortunately, none of the theorists whose work I have considered is quite as simplistically reductive as was Descartes or Zappa's high school teacher. In considering these various reductive strategies we are reminded that the aural properties of music have real physiological effects on listeners. While strong emotional responses to music cannot be explained solely in terms of these effects, we do well to keep them in mind. A further type of reductive strategy is to explain strong emotional responses to music, not with reference to sonic features of the music, but with reference to the psychology of affected listeners. Sometimes this type of explanation is made of individual listeners: "Jane always cries when that song comes on the radio because it reminds her of her brother"; or "Mike is a sensitive guy; that is why he cries at the opera." Sometimes quite general claims are made about listeners who respond strongly to music. Poizat, who studied Paris opera-goers, says that all "true" opera lovers cry; calm, dry-eyed opera fans are not fully engaged in the experience. Similarly, one might say that those who respond strongly to music are over-sensitive (which may be construed as a virtue or a vice), or that they lack the inhibitions which prevent other listeners from responding in a like manner, or that they have a stronger than average interest in music.

Is there any evidence that would allow us confidently to make general claims about those who seem to experience the sublime in music on a more regular basis than others? Again, the paucity of data limits the generality of our conclusions. Panksepp found that his female students were more likely to admit experiencing chills in response to music (especially to sad music) than were his male students. In his study of "everyday" uses of music listening, Sloboda also found that women were more likely than men to comment on the mood-altering or enhancing functions of music. Could it be that women are naturally more sensitive to emotion in music than men? Some brain studies suggest that women show less lateralization and more symmetrical representation of musical stimuli than do men. Yet it is just as plausible that the different types of responses to music which men and women seem to display are the result of cultural and social conditioning. The "gendering" of emotional work within a society and of appropriate aesthetic engagement are fascinating subjects worthy of separate books. Still other researchers report no difference in emotional responses to music between men and women. Suffice it to say that we can make no firm conclusions here about gender and emotional response to music.

Can any additional general claims be supported regarding people who tend to experience the sublime in music? What difference, if any, does musical training and involvement make? In the reports I have read and among the different people I have discussed these issues with I have found a wide range of possibilities. Some people with little or no musical training have strong emotional responses to music; professional musicians may appreciate music greatly on an intellectual level but have a rather detached emotional attitude to it. In a recent study comparing those who experienced chills in response to music and those who did not, both groups contained professional musicians, amateur musicians and non-musicians. A couple of studies have found a positive correlation between a subject's level of musical involvement (assessed by the importance of music in life and time spent listening to music) and incidences of strong emotional responses to music or a tendency to experience chills listening to music. But we have no way of knowing which factor here is the cause and which is the effect. Does experiencing strong emotions on listening to music make you value music more, or does valuing music highly facilitate strong emotional responses to it? Both possibilities seem plausible.

STRONG RESPONSES AND COGNITION

The obvious deficiency of the pharmaceutical model is that music, despite its capacity to produce tangible physical effects in listeners, is not a drug. We do not merely "react" to music, as we may simply react to loud noises or high pitches. We hear music with more or less adequate understanding, and our grasp of a musical work depends on a number of factors. These include our familiarity with the work, with its underlying tonal structure and with other music from the same culture or sub-culture. A more satisfactory explanation of strong emotional responses to music, then, would treat the music *as music* rather than as sound patterns. This has been done in two different ways: some have emphasized music's status as a cognitive object; others have stressed music's expressive and aesthetic features.

We saw earlier that Aristotle believed that music in the Phrygian mode triggered trance states. It is unlikely that Aristotle meant that music in this mode, simply understood as sound, would have induced a trance state. As a basic methodological rule ("the principle of charity") one should not attribute a clearly implausible thesis to a thinker without strong evidence that he accepts it. Rouget, who has made a careful study of the relevant texts, finds that Aristotle treats the

Phrygian mode as necessary, but not sufficient, to induce a trance. (That is, all melodies which induce a trance are in the Phrygian mode; but not all melodies in that mode induce trance states.) What is it then about the Phrygian mode that seems to gives it such distinctive power? According to Rouget's interpretation Aristotle treats the Phrygian mode as a coded signal. Music in this mode stands for Phrygia, the cradle of Dionysius worship and of the frenzied rites associated with trance states in ancient Greece. If Rouget's interpretation is correct, Aristotle's account is cognitive. Music is treated as something to be understood, not as a stimulus which automatically causes a response. Listeners who fail to recognize the Phrygian mode, or who do not grasp the association between the mode and Dionysian worship, will be not affected.

More recent cognitive accounts of strong emotional responses to music look not to music's potential for symbolism but to its underlying structure. As we saw earlier, various studies have indicated that such responses to music were often associated with certain musical-structural features. What these features seem to share is that most involve the violation of expectancies or implications. When we listen to a musical work, our hearing extends "backwards" - remembering the sequence of tones that has led to the present moment - as well as "forwards" - anticipating what is to come. Sometimes consciously, but usually unconsciously, we form expectations about the likely tonal and rhythmic patterns that are to follow. This is part of what it means to listen to music with understanding. When our expectations are violated in certain ways we may respond to the music with emotion. This kind of account is cognitive because it gives a central role to musical understanding. Anyone who failed to understand a musical excerpt - who was, say, unfamiliar with the underlying tonal structure and failed to have the right kind of expectations at the relevant junctures - would not find the music moving.

But a cognitive account that looks to the structural features of music is surely not the whole story. Musical works with similar structural features may sound very different from one another. Levinson for one has argued that these "structural" accounts need to be supplemented by attention to expressive and aesthetic considerations. Is the music any good? How well and how expressively is it played? Which emotions does it convey? What we seem to require in order to explain the potential of certain musical works to induce chills is some sort of narrative that spells out an underlying emotional scenario. Recall that Levinson found that much of the music associated with a chill response was poignant and bitter-sweet. This is no coincidence; it is by virtue of this poignancy that certain works provoke strong emotional responses. Levinson's comparison of Johannes Brahms's *String Quintet in G*, opus 111 with the roughly contemporary *Russian Easter Overture* by Nikolai Rimsky-Korsakov is illustrative here. While the opening movement of the first work affords a sustained chill experience, the latter seems "incapable" of inducing chills, despite being colourful, imbued with feeling and even absorbing. The reason for this is found in the character of the music itself. Bluntly put, the *Russian Easter Overture* seems to Levinson superficial. As he puts it, "Its energy does not speak to or tap into anything profound in human nature." Levinson is surely right in arguing that we need to pay attention to expressive and aesthetic considerations before we can explain why some music moves us. We may even grant him that it is music with a particular kind of expressive narrative - one that reflects certain truths about human existence - that is particularly affecting. Although we seem to be on the right track, we still do not have a satisfactory explanation. A larger problem looms: why is any music (as opposed to a particular sub-set of it) moving?

SUMMING UP AND MOVING FORWARD

None of the explanations for various strong responses to music we have considered has been wholly satisfying. What are the qualities of a good explanation more generally? Is there anything that all good philosophical and scientific explanations share? A number of criteria come to mind. First, such explanations are general rather than individual. Anne, one of the Parisian opera-lovers interviewed by Poizat, says that she responds with "physical ecstasy" only to the voice of Maria Callas. The explanation for her response may be interesting to uncover; but unless it can tell us something about others' responses more generally it is unlikely to hold any significance outside the circle of Anne's friends and family. Explaining Anne's reaction is as likely to tell us as much about Anne as it does about anything else. Second, a satisfactory explanation must attempt to "save the phenomena." That is, explanations which explain away or dismiss what is to be explained are unacceptable. A purported explanation of carpal tunnel syndrome which concluded that carpal tunnel syndrome is illusory or "all in the mind" of those suffering would not be satisfactory. I take it as given that strong emotional responses to music are genuine and require explanation. Furthermore, a satisfactory explanation should not point to something that *itself* requires an explanation. In other words, "magical" explanations are disallowed. For this reason accounts of strong emotional responses to music along the lines of "I cried because the music was beautiful" will have to be eschewed. In offering such an explanation all we have done is to shift the problem from the effects of a particular work to the power of beauty more generally, and now we are left with the considerable task of providing a non-circular explanation of why we respond with deep emotion to beauty. Finally, a satisfactory explanation should shed some light on the full compass of the phenomena under discussion. Sublime responses to music range from trance states to weeping to feelings of renewal. While some of these responses may be more recalcitrant to elucidation than others, each should fit somewhere within the larger explanatory structure.

On last thing: explanations need not be plausible or transparent to those affected. I would not be bothered if listeners found my explanations of their responses counterintuitive, any more than a dentist should be bothered if his patients reject tooth decay as an explanation of their toothache.

I propose a change of focus; if we are to make any headway on this problem we must shift the discussion. Rather than continue to consider why certain musical works or certain structural features of musical works can arouse experiences of the sublime we need to step back and consider some more basic questions. This means a move from particular works, performances and types of listeners to the nature of music more generally. The question of why certain musical works in certain contexts arouse experiences of the sublime in some listeners cannot be separated from the more fundamental (and more philosophically interesting) question of why any music in any context brings about experiences of the sublime in any listener.

This shift in focus is advantageous, perhaps even unavoidable, for a number of reasons. First, our investigation of the various musical works that are reported to invoke experiences of the sublime revealed that they may have little in common with one another. It is true that certain structural features of musical works and works with certain expressive characters arouse powerful feelings in listeners more reliably than do works with different structural features and expressive characters. Yet as reliably as these aspects of music can be tied to responses in listeners, there is too little stability and regularity here to construct a satisfactory explanation. For instance, there is nothing like the reliability we find between certain structural properties of works and judgements about the expressive *character* of music (as opposed to the expressive *effect* of such music). Different individuals react differently to the same music, and one individual's reaction to a particular work or performance may vary on different occasions. I do not mean to exaggerate the heterogeneity of music that has been said to evoke powerful responses in listeners. Certain musical works are cited again and again as capable of doing this. This fact is not a red herring; that is, there are likely reasons why it is the case. But investigating these works will provide only part of the story and is best carried out within an examination of the power of music more broadly construed.

Second, we have also seen that listeners who have strong emotional responses to music have little in common with one another. They do not share age, gender, cultural or professional background. Only quite general things can be said about them; for instance, that such listeners enjoy music and find it a valuable part of their lives. It is not even clear whether the value they place on music is a cause of their propensity to experience strong responses or an effect of it. Until further research is conducted, it seems unlikely that a satisfactory explanation could be built upon the personalities of affected listeners.

Finally, strong emotional responses to music have also been attributed to the artistic value of certain works. It is tempting to conclude that only the finest musical works (masterpieces or "works of genius") are capable of arousing powerful emotional responses in listeners. However, the empirical evidence does not bear this out, even when we allow a generous account of artistic value and recognize that works in different musical genres call for different evaluative criteria. Either we disregard the testimony of listeners who have been profoundly affected by less than great music, or we stretch the concept of artistic value to the point of emptiness. A more extended discussion of these matters will have to wait until a later chapter. At the moment I can say that considerations of value have a definite role to play, but their explanatory power is limited. "I cried because the music was beautiful," although perhaps true, will not suffice as an explanation. Before we can understand why beautiful music might make us cry, we have to understand why any music at all might do so.

6

EXPLAINING STRONG EMOTIONAL RESPONSES TO MUSIC II

MUSIC AND THE SOCIAL WORLD

HERE IS THE TASK AT HAND: explain why music is *generally* valued and moving to many people as a preliminary to making sense of the *particular* issue of why some music is extremely, even profoundly, moving. To do this, one of the central things we need to come to terms with is the idea that music and the experience of music are fundamentally social, rather than strictly personal or individual. But what exactly does this claim mean, and what implications might be drawn from it? The philosopher Ludwig Wittgenstein is well known for (among other things) his "private language argument," undercutting the idea that the meanings of the terms in a language might be known only by a single user. In a similar vein, yet without actually applying his argument to music, I hope to show that there could be no strictly private musical experience.

Human beings are social animals. Plato and Aristotle, among the earliest in the western tradition to address the peculiar nature of humankind, reject the idea that a human being could exist apart from a social order. Aristotle famously remarked that anyone living outside of a community would be "either subhuman or superhuman." A growing number of researchers provide an evolutionary perspective on these ancient philosophical speculations. They suggest that hominid brain expansion was driven largely by social factors. For example, face-to-face interaction places demands on working memory and may have been an influence on frontal lobe development. Furthermore, the grasp of symbolic relationships which makes language possible (and indeed language itself) could have proceeded from the need to manage the complexities of increasingly large social groups.

The recognition of music as a human (rather than a natural or supernatural) product goes hand-in-hand with its fundamentally social character. This can be seen in many ways. Music is created (composed, improvised, performed) by human beings, usually for the benefit of other human beings. Even in those cultures where unmediated natural sound can be considered music (and there are only very few of these), the grouping of natural sound with song or instrumental music is a social convention. The transmission of music from one generation to the next begins very early in life. Think of the universal practice of singing children to sleep, and the existence everywhere of a special musical repertory for children. Musical culture relies on human transmission. If a group were to disappear and leave behind no comprehensible record of its music-making, we would have no idea what its musical culture was like. Even musicians who are self-taught must rely on other human beings (or recordings of them) to grasp how their instruments are supposed to sound, not to mention how to make sounds into a musical work.

So far the connections I have noted between music and the social should be uncontroversial. Yet there are additional ways in which music is dependent on the social world and social realities. Most crucially, systems of musical meaning are conventional; that is, they rely on human agreement in a number of crucial ways. First, what counts as music in each society rests on cultural agreement. Random sounds are not music. Even in the case of avant-garde music that employs random sounds, human design or intention must enter at some stage. All societies place limits on music-making, such that certain sounds are accepted as musical while others are excluded. Human beings make music only in particular ways. The range of variety present in the world's musical cultures is considerably narrower than the scope of imaginable sound patterns. Similarly, the underlying patterns which give music meaning are also conventional. One cannot make music out of nothing. Musical resources - many musical instruments and some of their performance practices, the capacities of the human voice, rhythmic and tonal patterns - pre-exist individual musicians and composers. This is the case even as composers sometimes invent new musical instruments and challenge the capacities of the human voice. Different musical cultures are based on different patterns of tonal and rhythmic organization. Understanding the music of an unfamiliar culture requires familiarity with these underlying patterns, usually acquired through guided listening. These patterns of musical structure and meaning are social constructions which evolved though human musical practice. Composers who challenge the limits of their sub-culture's musical conventions must presuppose and engage with those conventions in order for their music to sound novel. Furthermore, by the time an individual's sound productions are considered music (even inferior music) rather than noise or mere sound, he will already have begun to assimilate the patterns of musical organization specific to his culture. A child's random banging on pots and pans is usually considered noise rather than music. However, if he sings a recognizable but out-of-tune melody, this has at least some claim to the status of music-making.

I should say here that just because a practice is conventional that does not entail that it is necessarily arbitrary. The original association between a red traffic light and the obligation to stop is arbitrary; however, once established, particular conventions may be followed for reasons of convenience or expediency. It makes sense for different jurisdictions to share the same traffic signal conventions to some extent. Still other conventions may have a basis in the nature of things. For example, the convention about the zero of the Kelvin temperature scale is backed by the postulate that there is no molecular activity below 0° K. So the claim that systems of music meaning are conventional does not entail the very different claim that they are wholly arbitrary. Indeed, they are probably not. The fact that we can come to understand the music of different cultures probably indicates that such systems have a natural basis in human auditory processing capacities. (Indeed, this is suggested by a great deal of research in both psychology and ethnomusicology.)

Now, some readers will think that I have stressed the obvious. Others may find my characterization of musical experience as fundamentally social to be counterintuitive. Before continuing it seems a good idea to address some objections to the account just laid out.

First, I mentioned in chapter 1 that music is often seen as other-worldly or as having some connection with a non-human spirit realm. Is it possible that in stressing so relentlessly music's status as a human and social artefact I have misconstrued its actual "essence" or under-valued it somehow? After all, there might be something about music which makes it vulnerable to "supernatural" interpretations. Is music so remarkable and marvellous that we do not want to believe that it is "merely" human? Yet the conception of music as partaking of the spiritual is matched by another ancient connection, that of music and the bodily, the sensual, the earthbound. The Greek goddess of wisdom, Athena, invented the aulos but threw it away because blowing into it distorted her facial features. Is this an analogy for the materiality and physicality of music-making, for its incompatibility with rational understanding? It was not for nothing that Tolstoy made the adulterous lovers in his novella *The Kreutzer Sonata* a pair of musicians, and has the cuckolded husband declare that sensuous music such as the Beethoven work named in the title should be forbidden by law. While music is used in worship, many religious groups in a number of traditions cir-cumscribe its use. From the earliest days of the Catholic Church to the end of the Middle Ages a very great number of edicts, bulls and even entire church councils were devoted to music and singing. It is also worth remembering that still life paintings in the *memento mori* and *vanitas* genre - pictures that aimed to remind viewers of their own mortality and of the worthlessness of earthly pleasures - often depicted musical instruments or sheet music.

There is another objection to the view that music is fundamentally social: music has important solitary and individual uses, and "social" and "individual" are opposites. Listening to music can seem like an escape from the social world. Surely many people have had the experi-ence of turning up the volume on their headphones in an attempt to drown out a nearby conversation. In his research using mass observa-tion studies, Sloboda found that listeners often used music to enhance their time alone, rather than to connect with others. The valued out-comes of such listening included the remembrance of past events and personal mood enhancement or alteration. These aims would seem to be self-referring, even solipsistic - but hardly social.

Nonetheless, the description of music as an escape from the social is misleading. For the character of an experience to be fundamentally social, it does not have to be social every single moment. Social is contrasted here, not with "private" but with "natural." What did the listeners who participated in Sloboda's study wish to remember when they listen to music? Most likely, a happy time spent in the company of others or with one special person. Mood enhancement or alteration, while affecting primarily the individual, can also make it easier for her to cope with the demands of social life. Indeed, one of the listeners Sloboda quotes says that she listens to music so that she can "wallow in self-pity" in order to "rejoin the world" later. Clearly, this is an example of the private use of music in pursuit of a social goal. The fact that music can have a private or individual use does not make it any less a social product. We are creatures of society; the fact that we sometimes want a break from other people (or from certain specific others) does not make us any less so. Communing with music is a form of communing with human reality, and that is social.

An analogy with the social basis of emotion can help here. Shame is "pain accompanied by the idea of some action of ours that we think that others censure." (I have quoted Spinoza's definition from his *Ethics* because it is both elegant and just.) The crucial point here - one that must be captured by any adequate definition of shame - is that the behaviour for which the agent feels shame is condemned by those around him. Typically, children are taught to feel shame for that behaviour of which their culture disapproves. Someone who grew up without this type of training would not feel the appropriate things at the appropriate time. Shame in the individual is only possible within a system of shared morality and a social context. It is true that one can privately feel shame, or feel shame for behaviour which no one else has yet noticed (but which others would condemn if they did notice). Yet none of this makes shame any less a social emotion.

Finally, am I guilty of an over-reductive strategy - of reducing music to the social, or claiming that it is "nothing but" a form of social interaction? The claim that music is social is an important claim, but not a reductive one. It leaves much more to be said about music and about our responses to it. Music is made (typically) in interaction with other musicians, with a score coded by others, with instruments made by others. The lone musician who makes her instrument, composes or improvises the music and performs for herself alone is a special case. What she does is understandable as music only if we connect her activities to our musical practice. Music is one of many social institutions that have a private or internalist counterpart; others include religion, morality, reading, and so on.

Before setting this issue aside let us consider some remarks by Bennett Reimer, a well-known authority on music education. He eloquently expresses what perhaps many have felt:

> Music is, in a certain sense, only one of a multitude of demonstrations of the subject-object interplay that characterizes human reality. But in another sense, music is a remarkably vivid and concentrated instance of the self-within-the-world human condition. Perhaps more fully than any other endeavor, music manifests selfness for the sheer sake of the human need to demonstrate selfness, and it does this with materials - sounds - that exist entirely and are employed sheerly for the sake of self-manifestation - self as instance of the universal human condition, as instance of the culturally determined human condition, as instance of the individuality of each human's condition.

Reimer's remarks clearly and forcefully express what I believe is a widely held though rarely articulated position. Reimer argues that music can be a means of self-expression. (I assume he has in mind here performing or perhaps broadcasting music; it is difficult to see how solitary listening to work composed and performed by others could be a demonstration of self-ness.) There is some plausibility to this way of understanding music; yet if it is to be made compelling, it has to be understood in a way that does not compromise music's social character. Perhaps this is why Reimer qualifies his remarks so carefully - he stresses that the self-expressive function of music is only *one* sense in which music can be understood.

Several things can be said about the view that music manifests selfness. First, we have seen that music is not made with "sounds." It is made with only a specific range of sounds which varies according to culture but never encompasses the full range of sounds that humans can make. In choosing the sounds with which to make music, the performer is necessarily participating in a social or cultural activity. He is choosing over a range that others have specified. If he does not, then his "music" is not likely to be understood as such by others, and although his behaviour may be expressive of self, it is debatable whether it is an instance of music-making.

Second, there is one clear sense in which music is a manifestation of self. Nothing says "Here I am" like a solitary voice raised in song or the tones of an instrument. These demand the interest and attention of others. (If you are sceptical, try singing loudly in a crowded place and notice the attention you receive.) A scene from the classic film *Casablanca*, set during the Second World War, is relevant here. Much of the film takes place at Rick's "Café American," where one of the house rules is "no politics." One night a group of Nazi officers take over the piano and loudly sing together "Watch on the Rhine," a German patriotic song. Their message is clear: "We're here. Get used to it." If this were not their message, their singing would not be the threat that it is perceived to be and would not demand a response. Yet expressions or manifestations of self are rarely *for* the self; they are for others. Music-making demands recognition. It says "Here I am," but it also says "[You] listen to me." So whatever the self-expressive capacities and character of music, these cannot be understood separately from its social nature.

MUSIC AND SOCIAL BONDING

Can we draw any other implications from music's social character? How does music contribute to social bonding - to the formation and sustaining of human relations? Three types of social bonds are important here: mutual bonds between caregivers and infants; pair bonds between adults; and bonds linking members of social groups and sub-groups.

"Attachment" is a technical term used in psychology. It refers to the intense reciprocal relationship and systems of behaviour between an infant and a caregiver, generally its mother. Attachment behaviour is found in non-human animals, including primates, rats, voles, sheep, and many others. Indeed, to be a mammal is to be, from birth, socially dependent and bonded to others. Caregivers who are strongly bonded to their (at times very demanding) infants are more likely to strive to secure their infants' survival, even at great inconvenience to themselves. There is a good deal of evidence from a variety of sources that musical activity facilitates and reinforces attachment between human infants and their caregivers. In fact, of all of the proposed evolutionary functions of music, that of contributing to infant survival has the most empirical support. For one thing, there is no evidence of any culture, past or present, in which caregivers have not sung to infants on a regular basis; and the style of infant-directed singing tends to be one of heightened emotional expressiveness. It is well known that parents the world over speak in a characteristic musical manner to babies - more slowly, rhythmically and repetitively, with elevated pitch, simplified pitch contours and an expanded pitch range. This way of speaking (variously called "motherese," "parentese" and "infant-directed speech") has been documented in numerous languages and cultures, among mothers, fathers, children and even those with no childcare experience. As for the infants on the receiving end of this musical speech, they show more positive affect in response to infant-directed rather than adult-directed speech and singing. When babies are presented with audiovisual versions of their mothers' speech and singing, they exhibit more sustained interest in the singing than in the speech. Furthermore, live maternal singing has a more enduring effect on infant arousal than does live maternal speech. Babies' preference for singing over speaking would seem to be innate, as it is found even among infants born to congenitally deaf parents, who neither sing nor speak. Taken together, these findings indicate that mothers singing to children may have been one of the earliest human forms of musical interaction. It is reasonable to suppose that such behaviour persists the world over because it contributed to infant-caregiver bonding and thus to infant survival.

Just as music appears to contribute to bonding between infants and their caregivers, it is likely that it also contributes to pair bonds between adults. Music is used to facilitate romantic interaction the world over. When I first attended a singing class and was exposed to a number of songs from different traditions and historical periods, I was struck by how many of them were about love or related love stories. Darwin believed that music caused emotional responses in listeners because of its use in courtship. But it is just as likely that the reverse is true - music is used in courtship because of its capacity to cause emotional responses.

Animal studies, including the very large body of research on birdsong, also indicate that music encourages and strengthens pair bonds. It is an interesting philosophical question whether the "music" made by various non-human animals - from birds to apes to whales - fulfils the relevant criteria to count as music. If it does, then we can with greater confidence extend what we know about animal music and related behaviour to the human context. To be sure, some cultures have grouped the music-like sounds made by various animals together with human music-making activities. But usage in this case does not settle the issue. By the same token, we must not beg the question against the possibility of animal music by starting with an over-restrictive definition. Traditionally, the songs of birds have had the greatest claim to being considered music. Many reasons have been offered, but two seem to come up again and again: birdsong is complex, and it is learned rather than innate. These features are shared by the vocalizations of some marine mammals, but not by the calls of frogs, crickets and other insects. So we have to be quite careful in drawing implications about human musicality from these simpler unlearned calls; but we can with greater confidence extrapolate and extend what we know about more complex animal vocalizations to human beings.

Gibbons (also called "lesser apes") are very agile, tree-dwelling primates that live in Asian rainforests. Unlike their relatives the great apes (including chimpanzees and orang-utans) they form pair bonds and have a monogamous social structure. Gibbons produce "loud and long" song bouts, most often in the early morning. Ten of the twelve currently recognized gibbon species duet, usually in mated pairs. There is some evidence from research with one of the dueting species (siamangs) that dueting strengthens the pair bond. Singing together seems to be positively correlated with grooming activity and behavioural synchronization, and negatively correlated with inter-individual distance between mates. It is interesting to note that among all singing primates both the female and male sing, and in most species dueting also occurs. All primates known to sing also have a monogamous social structure. Gibbons' "songs" do not seem to be learned or complex, so we have to be cautious in extrapolating from gibbons to humans. However, studies of birdsong, which does fulfil the criteria for music, point to similar conclusions about dueting and pair bonds. Among birds, dueting occurs mainly in monogamous species. This suggests that the evolution of singing in primates and duet singing more generally is somehow related to the evolution of monogamy. Since the four groups of primates that sing (and duet) are not closely related, it is considered possible that singing (and dueting) evolved four times among primates.

The most distinctive difference between human music and the sound productions of other primates is that humans are able to keep to a steady beat. A regular beat makes for a better coordinated song, with more singers able to participate. Among our early hominid ancestors, well-coordinated vocalizations may have made for a more effective display than an uncoordinated jumble of voices, thereby providing a deterrent to potential attackers. It is also likely that groups which were able to sing together would have been able to cooperate and coordinate in other ways as well. Music is still used to facilitate coordination within groups - think of the music that accompanies marches in formation and the music played in exercise classes. Music is also effective in coordinating and promoting the solidarity of groups in less literal ways. Sociologists confirm (as parents and teachers have probably already suspected) that teenagers use music to signal group allegiance. National anthems and hymns are also relevant here. Singing or listening together to a national anthem (or any song strongly symbolic of a particular group identity) can make individuals identify with larger social entities. Surely such identification is part of what is going on when burly men at sporting events weep when they hear, say, the Welsh national anthem.

Remember the scene from *Casablanca* that I mentioned earlier? Just before, we saw Yvonne, a young French woman, come into Rick's café

on the arm of a German officer, raising the ire of a French acquaintance. Later that evening a group of Nazis gather round the piano and
affirm their group identity by loudly singing "Watch on the Rhine."
The atmosphere is tense. Acting quickly, Victor Laszlo, a resistance
leader, persuades the café's dance band to play "La Marseillaise." Soon,
almost everyone else in the café, including Yvonne, is singing along and
drowning out the Germans. We see a close-up of Yvonne in tears, and
at the end of the song she shouts "Vive la France!" Hearing and singing
"La Marseillaise" has reaffirmed her own group identity and reawak-
ened her loyalty to France. The music succeeds where the appeals of a
fellow French citizen could not.

MUSIC, EMOTION AND THE BRAIN: (1) GENERAL

> Why the keening sounds from Mississippi should strike notes of
> thrill and terror and wonder in hearts in the suburbs of London, I
> don't know. It can only be because it goes beyond colour, blood - it
> goes to the bone.
>
> Keith Richards

There is no neat or tidy story to be told about music's effect on the brain.
The nature of emotion itself continues to be a matter of fierce debate
among scholars in a number of fields, including philosophy, biology and
brain sciences, and anthropology and the social sciences. All serious
researchers interested in music, emotion and the brain acknowledge
the paucity of evidence ("a few peppercorns" as Panksepp puts it) and
recognize that work has barely begun. So the story that I tell here will
have to be provisional, conjectural and fragmentary. Emotions would
seem to involve the body, its brain and the mind; that is, (at least some)
emotions are felt in the body, recognized by or known in the mind and
mediated by various brain systems. It is important to note that there
is not one single "emotion centre" or system in the brain. Our current
understanding is that emotional circuits are widely distributed, forming a tree-like structure in the brain. The roots and trunk-lines are in
deeper subcortical areas, with branches intersecting to form "wide can-
opies" in the evolutionarily more recent cerebral cortex or neocortex. It

is likely that music penetrates these emotional systems at many levels, from the auditory cortex (where basic auditory processing of all types is carried out) through to evolutionarily more primitive areas in the subcortex. This helps us to understand how it is that the emotional power of music can be at once cognitive (relating to patterns of musical expectation and the recognition of extra-musical associations) and non-cognitive (acting on deeper brain regions). As Richards puts it in the epigraph to this section, music goes "to the bone."

Some researchers believe that music's ability to affect our mood - the emotional charge it can deliver - is derived from the dynamic aspects of brain systems that normally control the emotions of our "extra-musical" lives. Some interesting research supports this contention. The amygdala is a set of neurons located deep in the brain's temporal lobes. It has several functions related to the processing of emotions, especially those related to threat and danger. Patients with bilateral amygdala damage have trouble recognizing unpleasant emotions in facial expressions. They can typically recognize, say, happiness, but not fear, in another's face. In one study, fifty-six musical excerpts were composed with the intention of inducing or expressing happiness, sadness, peacefulness or fear, as if the music was to be part of a film soundtrack. All of the excerpts followed the rules of diatonic tonality (the western tonal system). The participants in the study - sixteen who had undergone right or left temporal lobe resection including the complete removal of the amygdala for the relief of epilepsy, and sixteen unaffected controls - listened to the musical excerpts and were asked to judge according to a nine-point scale to what degree each of the four emotions was expressed. Participants in the control group had little trouble distinguishing among scary, happy and peaceful excerpts, although sad and peaceful selections were sometimes confused. The participants with brain injuries were almost as adept at recognizing which excerpts were intended to express happiness, but there were considerably worse at correctly identifying the scary excerpts. Patients with damage to the right temporal lobe seemed to perform particularly poorly, often selecting the label "peaceful" for the scary music, a mistake never made by the controls. The investigators ruled out the possibility that the patients with brain injuries may have been unable to judge the emotional character of the music due to more general perceptual deficiencies. All performed at a very high level - as well as the control group - on a separate error-detection test that used the same musical excerpts. While we can at present only speculate how or why, it would seem that the same neural mechanisms that allow us to recognize fear in an actor's facial expressions may also allow us to perceive the expression of fear in the music of the accompanying soundtrack.

We have evidence from a number of sources that music affects the brain directly. Music brings about a variety of measurable physical responses in listeners, including heightened awareness, alertness and excitement. A study by the Yale School of Medicine showed that patients who listened to music of their choice on headphones during surgery required much less sedation than control groups who listened to white noise or did not wear headphones. Another study found that listening to music in the early stages after a stroke can improve a patient's memory. Patients who listened to music for a couple of hours a day were found to have a better recovery of memory and attention skills compared to patients who listened only to audio books or to nothing at all. The music group also showed a more positive general frame of mind and were less likely to be depressed or confused. The researchers were not sure why music had these particular effects on the brain. They speculate that music might have directly stimulated recovery in the damaged areas, or it might have stimulated more general mechanisms that helped the brain repair its own neural networks. Another possibility is that the music may have acted specifically on the parts of the nervous system implicated in feelings of memory, pleasure and reward.

The neurologist Oliver Sacks has written movingly about his patients with neurological disorders who are given a respite from their condition through music. He describes one patient with Parkinson's disease who tended to remain completely motionless for hours a day; she regained ease and fluency of movement when she played the piano, heard or even imagined music. Another was able to regain the use of her apparently paralysed leg through music therapy after conventional physiotherapy had failed. That music may act directly on the brain to harmful effect is indicated by the phenomenon of musicogenic epilepsy - seizures induced by hearing or (in very rare cases) imagining music.

Some of the most remarkable findings about music and the brain have come from the neurologist Isabelle Peretz's work with her patient IR. When IR was 28 she suffered bilateral cerebral damage due to the repair of cerebral aneurysms. One of the consequences of her brain damage is amusia, an umbrella term that refers to various forms of music-related perceptual and productive deficiencies. Before she had brain surgery IR used to sing, but today she can no longer sing a note, and she fails to recognize once familiar melodies. Peretz and her colleagues found that although IR fails basic music recognition tests (such as judging whether two melodies played in succession are the same or different), her ability to judge the emotional tone of melodies has been remarkably spared. She performs normally in tests to judge whether a melody is happy or sad. How can this be? One possibility Peretz suggests is that emotional and non-emotional judgements about music are the product of distinct neural pathways. There is already a body of evidence suggesting that certain aspects of facial identity and facial expression are analysed separately by the brain. Brain injury can result in deficits in the recognition of facial identity (judging whether two faces are the same or different) while sparing recognition of facial emotion (judging whether a face is happy or sad). The reverse is also possible - patients can lose the ability to judge facial emotion while retaining the capacity for facial recognition. The existence of separate neural pathways for emotional and non-emotional judgements of music would also help explain how it is that some who suffer from brain injuries complain that music has come to sound "flat" or without emotion, while retaining basic recognitional abilities (sometimes called "anhedonic amusia").

Evidence of a different sort for music's effect on the brain comes from tests using positron emission tomography (PET) to examine patterns of cerebral blood flow during affective responses to music. In this type of test a radioactive substance is injected into the bloodstream, and the emission of positrons - tiny particles emitted during the decay of the radioisotope - is measured. In this way the activity in different regions of the brain can be measured and visualized. Researchers in Montreal scanned ten volunteers as they listened to a novel musical passage that contained different degrees of dissonance. They found patterns of brain activation in several distinct brain areas already known to be involved in the processing of emotion. The fact that dissonance in the music was associated with certain positive or negative emotional ratings suggests that the regions affected were involved specifically in response to these emotions. Later research by members of the same team used PET scans to examine brain activation in response to music that elicited chills. They found blood flow increases and decreases in brain regions thought to be involved in reward and motivation, emotion and arousal, including certain subcortical areas. Interestingly, the same brain regions are known to be active in response to other euphoria-inducing stimuli, such as food, sex and drugs of abuse.

There is one reason to interpret these studies with circumspection: the individuals tested had at least some level of musical training. Those in the first study were amateur musicians (it is not clear to what level of accomplishment) and those in the second study had at least eight years' training. So it is far from clear what these tests might reveal about non-musicians. However, the results of these studies have been confirmed and indeed extended by other researchers who tested non-musicians - subjects who had never learned singing or an instrument and who had no more musical education than the derisory amount offered in schools. These later experiments have a further advantage in that they used function magnetic resonance imaging (fMRI), which offers better spatial resolution than do PET scans. Researchers were for the first time able to document the involvement of the nucleus accumbens (NAc) during pleasant experiences of listening to music. Activity in this area and in other "reward-processing" regions strongly indicates an association between at least some experiences of listening to music and release of the neurotransmitter dopamine.

Remember Sacks' patients who gained some respite from their conditions by listening to music? It was later found that the drug L-dopa, which increases dopamine levels in the brain, had a beneficial effect. Today the drug is used routinely in the management of Parkinson's disease.

MUSIC, EMOTION AND THE BRAIN:
(2) THE NEUROBIOLOGY OF ATTACHMENT

So far we have discussed the different brain structures implicated in emotion. Emotional responses in the brain also involve different kinds of chemical release. These can be divided into hormones, which are released by the endocrine glands to work elsewhere in the body, and neurotransmitters. Neurotransmitters are chemical messengers which transmit information from one neuron to another. (Confusingly, the same substance can act as a hormone in the body and a neurotransmitter in the brain.) Neurons in the subcortical regions of the hypothalamus, basal forebrain and brainstem release chemicals that act in several higher brain regions to transform the working of neural circuits there. These chemicals include noradrenaline, which helps set in motion the fight-or-flight response; endorphins, involved in the muting of pain; and oxytocin, the "mothering hormone" (about which more below). Different emotions are produced by different (mainly subcortical) brain systems, and different emotions involve different patterns of neural activation.

We have seen that music can facilitate the formation of bonds between infants and caregivers, and adult pairs, and within larger social groups. This may be an accidental characteristic of music, or of humans, or both. Yet there are good reasons to suspect otherwise. In particular, attention to the neurobiological foundations of attachment is interesting here. Now, you might wonder if such a move can only be crudely reductive. Do I mean that love and attachment are nothing but neurological reactions? No. Human love - whether for one's children, partner, God or country - is clearly a complex, multifaceted phenomenon. Analysis of brain chemistry is not likely to provide anything like a full or satisfactory account. It is only a single piece of a much larger puzzle, but nonetheless a piece we would be unwise to disregard.

One of the most important hormones involved in both mother-child attachment and adult pair bonding is oxytocin. Panksepp, whose work on chills we looked at in the previous chapter, predicts on the basis of animal research that oxytocin and the opioid systems (part of what we have already referred to loosely as the brain's "reward regions") may turn out to be of crucial importance in the production and control of chills. Oxytocin (not to be confused with the prescription painkiller oxycontin) is manufactured in the brain (hypothalamus) and the body (ovaries or testes) of humans and other mammals. It is released by both men and women during sexual stimulation and orgasm, and by women during childbirth and lactation. It also is involved in a host of social and affiliative behaviour. Researchers have found that injecting animals with oxytocin induces behaviour associated with social bond formation, including grooming and mothering behaviour. For example, sheep and rats avoid their offspring after the postpartum period. But when these animals are given oxytocin, it causes them to seek contact with their young and produces other species-typical caretaking behaviour. Further evidence comes from the study of voles or meadow mice, rodents perhaps best known for causing damage to crops and golf courses. Prairie voles and montane moles are closely related, but have very different patterns of social organization. Prairie voles form long-term monogamous pairs and show high levels of parental care. Montane moles are polygamous, males and females do not share nests or a home range, and little time is invested in the care of young. While oxytocin levels are similar in both species, and oxytocin receptors are found in the brains of both, the distribution of the receptors is very different. In prairie voles (but not in montane moles) the receptors are found in the "reward regions" of the brain, where addictive drugs act. As one of the researchers put it, "When a monogamous vole mates, it is as if it got a hit of cocaine. The vole becomes addicted to whomever he was mating with."

Hypotheses about the links between oxytocin, music and social bonding would be difficult or even unethical to test on humans; but research with animals can provide important insight. Working with domestic chicks, whose vocal activities are well within human range, Panksepp and his colleagues have seen some dramatic and consistent results of the effects of music on these animals. It is worth noting that none of these results has been duplicated using white noise or human voices, although Panksepp is careful to say that he does not believe the chicks "appreciate" the music in anything like a human sense! When chicks are briefly isolated, music effectively reduces their separation cries. Since separation distress is alleviated by infusions of oxytocin and by molecules that activate certain receptors of the opioid system, Panksepp anticipates that music may also activate these brain systems. This hypothesis cannot be tested directly because of the difficulties in examining the synaptic release of neurotransmitters in such small animals. However Panksepp notes that music can also produce some simple fixed-action patterns in chicks - exactly the same types of fixed-action patterns evoked by infusions of oxytocin into the chick brain.

So far we have seen evidence that bonding between parents and infants, and between adult sexual partners, is mediated by oxytocin. What of social bonding on a larger scale, among members of a social group, such as those who joined in singing "La Marseillaise" in Rick's café? The neurologist Walter Freeman, again largely on the basis of animal studies, suspects that the same neurochemical mechanisms which support sexual reproduction and parent-child attachment may also form the neural basis for wider social cooperation. Freeman argues that human brains are literally solipsistic - in mutual isolation. Freeman and his students examined the path of neural activity in the rabbit brain accompanying and following an odour stimulus. By the time the signal had been transmitted to the cerebral cortex, they found that stimulus-dependent activity had vanished and was replaced by a new pattern of cortical activity. They found similar results in the visual, auditory and somatic areas of the cortex. Freeman's hypothesis is that the individualized patterns of activity, created by the chaotic dynamics of the cortices, reflect the experiences, contexts and significance of the stimuli for each individual. The "solipsism" of brains is not metaphysical (such that all that exists is a projection of one's own mind), but epistemological (such that knowledge is created in the brains of individuals).

Yet this will not do, as Freeman recognizes, since brains did not evolve as isolated units, but in social groups. Knowledge does not remain in individual brains but is shared, discussed and tested by larger groups. How is this possible? As Freeman puts it, "This problem lies not in translating or mapping knowledge from one brain to another but rather in establishing mutual understanding and trust through shared actions during which brains create the channels, codes, agreements, and protocols that precede that reciprocal mappings of information in dialogues." Freeman's answer (in brief) is that certain neurotransmitters, including oxytocin and endorphins, "dissolve" the solipsistic border and make possible the trust required for mutual action. He sees concrete examples of such dissolution in the trance states brought about by religious rituals in pre-literate societies, and in the psychological dislocation prized by attendees at large rave concerts in the developed West. In both cases music and dance serve as the "biotechnology" of group formation.

MUSIC AND THE MIND: COGNITIVE APPROACHES

We saw earlier that a common characteristic of strong emotional responses to music was the listener's complete or near-complete absorption in the music. Indeed, it would seem that absorption in the music is a defining characteristic of a strong response, as a readily distracted listener could hardly be said to be undergoing a "strong" experience or to be deeply moved. Attention to the character of such absorption also points us in the direction of music's social character. The work of the cognitive scientist William Benzon is particularly interesting in this regard. Benzon's focus of attention is the loss of self experienced by musicians during particularly intense concentration in performance, but his thoughts are also relevant to understanding listeners' experience. In line with much current and past philosophical reflection on the nature of the self, Benzon conceives of the self as a social construct which manages a complex of roles and statuses. One crucial way in which the self accomplishes this task is through inner speech, our common-sense understanding of thinking. Here Benzon draws on the psychologist Lev Vygotsky's classic work *Thought and Language*. Vygotsky's basic idea is that as children acquire language they gradually also begin to use internal speech to direct their activities. You may have noticed that children of a certain age often talk out loud to themselves as they play, describing what they are doing and indicating what they will do next. As a child's command of language grows, this self-directed speech becomes internal. Of course, this does not mean that the standard condition of encultured adults is to have internal speech going on all the time! Internal speech is just one of the ways (albeit a crucial one) in which the composite aspects of a self are managed. It can be turned off, if not completely at will then with some practice, in meditation. It also ceases during activities which require or elicit complete or near-complete absorption.

Benzon argues that during fluent musical performance, when the music seems to "flow" with little effort, the performer's self-directed speech ceases; it no longer plays a role in directing her activity. It is tempting to think that a similar process occurs when we are fully absorbed in listening to music. Inner speech ceases and its place is taken by music. Hence one social process (speech) is replaced by another (music). While music and language are both social in character, music is public in a way that internal speech is not. I can choose whether or not to share the content of my inner speech. However, if two or more people are absorbed in the same music, then the inner speech which constitutes their separate selves has ceased and is replaced by the representational content of the music. So absorption in music can make people set aside, however briefly, the things that separate them and share a common focus. This is the cognitive complement to the neurobiological story told in the previous section.

What about a solitary listener? He too sets aside the self's controlling narrative and replaces it with music. Music is, as I have been stressing, a social phenomenon. It thus brings a solitary listener into contact with others. We saw in chapter 3 that many listeners are consciously and explicitly reminded of music's human aspects when they are especially moved; they report feelings of commiseration, warmth and gratitude towards composers and, depending on the musical genre, towards performers. What about those listeners who experience music as otherworldly rather than as a human product, who feel that they are moved by nothing but the sheer beauty of the music? One possibility is that they are responding to the beauty in the music's expressive character. Music is often heard as expressing emotion. Any ascription of emotion to an inanimate object such as music relies on a primary or foundational understanding of human emotion. In responding to the music's emotional force, then, listeners are responding to something that puts it in the human (and thus social) domain.

To sum up briefly: powerful emotional responses to music both require and summon absorption in the music. During such absorption private internal speech is replaced by music, another socially constructed and socially mediated mental content. A significant feature of music is its capacity to convey emotion. Music's expressive potential constitutes a direct link between the musical and the social and is one more piece in the puzzle we are putting together. How is it that music is able to strike "notes of thrill and terror and wonder" in listeners' hearts?

MUSIC AND SOCIAL BONDING (AGAIN): INTIMACY

I have been building a case that music's social character accounts for its capacity to arouse experiences of the sublime in listeners. Yet have I simply replaced one mystery with another? Why, after all, should the social character of music have anything to do with its capacity to arouse strong emotions? I hope that I have provided some elements of the answer in the previous sections of this chapter. Music affects the body, brain and mind in ways that connect listeners in groups and take solitary listeners out of themselves, however briefly; and it is within social relations that we undergo some of the strongest and most significant emotional experiences of our lives. But all social relations are not equally important. Some elicit little attachment and emotion from participants, while others are profoundly significant with great capacity to move. Think, for example, of the different types of emotional bonding between members of an immediate family, colleagues in an office and buyers at an auction. Each of these groupings is "social," but there are great differences between them in emotional affiliation and levels of interdependence and trust. Generally, and other things being equal, the more intimate a relationship, the greater its capacity to influence the emotional lives of the participants. But what exactly is intimacy, and does it play a role in art appreciation? The answers to these questions will help us understand experiences of music and the sublime.

When we think of "intimacy," probably what comes most readily to mind are intimate relationships, but experiences and events can also be intimate. "Intimate" is often used simply as a synonym for "sexual," but that is misleading. Sexual acts may of course be intimate, but this is not necessarily the case. Think of rape or of commercial sex. Intimacy can, of course, have a physical component, but it need not. Non-sexual relationships may also be intimate. The closeness of intimacy can be psychic as well as physical, or rather than physical. There can be intimacy between platonic friends, between parents and children, between a doctor and a patient, and between a therapist and a client. In the Judeo-Christian tradition the relationship between worshippers and the Deity is often conceived of as intimate (an "I-Thou" relation).

The philosopher Robert Gerstein, in a much quoted article, has argued that intimacy requires privacy. If this is true, then we should hesitate to say that strong emotional experiences of music are intimate, as they happen to listeners who are part of groups as well as to solitary listeners. However while it may be that many intimate experiences require privacy, it does not seem to be invariably the case. Gerstein's example of prayer as an intimate act indicates that intimacy does not in fact require privacy. Prayer would seem to be no less genuine for being shared or communal. One additional aspect of Gerstein's analysis is particularly noteworthy: privacy is important for intimacy because the agent must be absorbed in the experience and fully participating. The presence of observers is likely to take him out of the moment, make him feel self-conscious and threaten the intimacy. This characteristic of intimate experiences - that they are absorbing and call forth participants' full involvement - is something that seems also to be true of strong emotional responses to music.

To say that a relationship or an encounter was "intimate" is to value it in some way, and intimate experiences and relationships hold significance for those participating. Intimacy has both cognitive and affective aspects. The feeling of intimacy is one of closeness, to the point even of union or striving towards union. The most important cognitive component of intimacy is the lowering or relaxation of personal boundaries and defences. This relaxation may be more or less consciously willed. Sometimes the first step to intimacy with another person is a conscious decision allowing oneself to be vulnerable. A perennial trope of Hollywood movies and popular fiction is the seemingly tough character who has been hurt or betrayed in the past and must now "open his heart" and "learn to love again." Yet in other contexts - and I am thinking particularly of infant-caregiver bonding - there is very little conscious or voluntary decision-making. Boundaries are lowered without one's express consent, indeed, sometimes even in opposition to one's wishes. You see the helpless infant, hormones do their work and no defence is possible!

Can encounters with artworks also be intimate? Ted Cohen is one of the few philosophers to have considered the links between art appreciation and intimacy. Treating jokes as artworks, he claims that joking is productive of intimacy between teller and audience. Cohen defines intimacy as "the shared sense of those in a community." This definition - even if it is correct - seems too general. But Cohen has hit on something important in his claim that our propensity to share aesthetic experiences (including, but not limited to, experiences of jokes) is linked with human beings' social or communal nature. He writes that we need reassurance that "something" in us - the something that is amused by a joke, awed by a beautiful sunset or moved by a poem - also constitutes an element of our common humanity. He writes: "I discover something of what it is to be a human being by finding this thing in me, and then having it echoed in you, another human being." When we are moved by music and want to share the music and the feeling with others, this can be the foundation of a deeper relationship. Yet if I am correct, listening to music can be an intimate experience even if the listener does not share his responses with others. How can this be? Furthermore, intimacy is a relational property; this is to say, one thing is intimate with another. So what is intimate with what in strong emotional experiences of music?

There are at least three possible answers to this question. Each indicates a different way in which the experience of music could be an intimate one, capable of moving listeners. The first is found in the kind of listening experience described by the philosopher Jerrold Levinson. Listening to music can mimic or be analogous to engagement in an intimate relationship. This happens when we empathetically experience the sounds presented, mirror the feelings expressed in the music and imagine that these feelings express another individual's authentic emotional experience. Levinson aptly describes such listening experiences as a form of "emotional communion." He writes: "we are in effect imagining that we are sharing in the precise emotional experience of another human being, the man or woman responsible for the music we hear." Such an experience of music carries with it "the sense of intimate contact with the mind and soul of another, the sense that one is manifestly not alone in the emotional universe." I certainly feel that I have had the type of experience that Levinson describe, and I would imagine that many others have as well. As we saw earlier, many listeners who experience the sublime in music do in fact connect their strong emotional responses with thoughts and feelings about composers. There is evidence that fans of musical genres in which the composer is less prominent (popular music, jazz and folk music, for example) will be more likely to attribute to performers the feelings expressed in the music. Hearing music in this way only "mimics" or is "analogous to" an intimate relationship because any relation between a listener and music is necessarily one-sided. Listeners may be intimate with music, but it sounds strained and implausible to say that music is intimate with listeners.

An experience of intimacy - even mimicry or an analogue of such an experience - can be powerfully emotional. The strong emotions generated by intimacy, whether that intimacy is inspired by music or by people close to us, are not always pleasant. Intimacy with another person means sharing their sorrows and disappointments as well as their joys. The feelings expressed by a composer in his or her music may not always be welcome; indeed, such feelings can even disturb us. For some listeners, the music of Richard Wagner is a case in point. His music has millions of admirers, yet others while recognizing the artistic achievement that his work represents remain deeply ambivalent about it because of the composer's well-known anti-Semitism and the associations between his music and Nazism. Daniel Levitin, formerly a session musician and record producer and currently a cognitive neuroscientist who studies music, expresses lucidly what I suspect are the inchoate feelings of many more listeners:

> Wagner has always disturbed me profoundly, and not just his
> music, but also the *idea* of listening to it. I feel reluctant to give

into the seduction of music created by so disturbed a mind and so dangerous (or impenetrably hard) a heart as his, for fear that I might develop some of the same ugly thoughts. When I listen to the music of a great composer I feel that I am, in some sense, becoming one with him, or letting a part of him inside me.

Music can play this role - it can allow us access to the heart and mind of another and be regarded as a vehicle of authentic emotional experience - only because of its intrinsically social character. To put it otherwise, if the "expression" of emotion in music were individual and private, we might still attribute the emotion to the composer, but we would not see ourselves as capable of sharing in it. We would certainly not use words like "emotional communion" and "intimacy" to describe what we feel.

There is a second way in which listening to music, whether alone or with others, can be an intimate experience. A number of writers have noted how our relationship with artworks can resemble our relationships with people. One aspect of this is that we can become attached to artworks just as we can become attached to people. For whatever reason, we may want to read a particular poem or hear a particular musical work at a particular time. The substitution of a different poem or piece of music would just not be the same; it would not give us the feeling or experience that we seek. This is comparable to the way in which you may wish to see a particular film or share a joke or anecdote with a particular friend whom you know will especially appreciate it. Having the experience with anyone else, even with another friend, would be much less satisfying. Two researchers (Panksepp and Bernatzky) go so far as to suspect that the bonds that attach listeners to the music that moves them has underlying neurobiological similarities to the love that people feel for one another. If the idea of "attachment" to musical works and performances is taken seriously, then it is but a small step to the idea that listeners can be (one-sidedly) intimate with music. And just as intimacy with another person involves lowering boundaries and defences, so too can intimacy with music. Again, Levitin puts this point extremely well: "To a certain extent - we surrender to music when we listen to it - we allow ourselves to trust the composers and musicians with a part of our hearts and our spirits; we let the music take us somewhere outside of ourselves." Listeners who experience more or less strong responses to music have let the music get past their defences, even to the point that they might be overwhelmed.

Finally, solitary listening to music can be an intimate experience such that the listener is intimate with himself. More concretely, different aspects of the self are brought together and reintegrated through engagement with music. Earlier in this chapter I explored the idea that the self was a complex of roles and statuses, managed by internal speech. Each of us, every day, must respond to different sets of demands and play different roles. Sometimes simultaneously and sometimes in sequence, one person may play the role of citizen, friend, parent, employee, mentor or witness. The need to balance one's internal life with the public self currently on display is ever present. Inner speech is one of the means by which we accomplish this. When we listen to music and let it dominate our minds, inner speech ceases and is replaced by music. Competing voices with rival demands are silenced through an intense focus on an external phenomenon. Yet although the music is external in the sense that it does not emanate from the listener's inner being, it is neither foreign nor alien. If the listener has chosen the music, then he is likely to be familiar with it. Even if the listener has not previously heard a particular work, he is likely to be familiar with the underlying tonal patterns and is able to follow it. And although some music is more readily comprehensible than other music, none can be totally foreign or completely unfamiliar. Music creates its own world of sound while remaining a human product. This is to say, music is the result of human ingenuity and construction, shaped by human patterns of organization and suited to the cognitive capacities of human beings, all for human purposes.

Music is extremely well suited to the task of providing a commanding internal focus and facilitating the reintegration of the self. It has certain features which make it particularly attractive and deserving as an object of intense external focus. One of these features is music's structure as developing and unfolding across time. Music and the various forms of artistic narrative (stage drama, epic poetry, short stories, novels and dance narratives, among others) share the fundamental feature of all being arts of time. As such, they present themselves as temporal gestalts, demanding continuous and continued attention. In this they are different from the visual arts; paintings and drawings exist in time, but they do not occupy time. Music and narratives, in contrast, fill up time; they impose an organization on time. The listener hears the unfolding of the musical narrative, but also becomes involved with it or swept up by it. He wants to know what will happen next. One mark of a bad story is that we can stop listening or reading at any point - we don't care how things will turn out. Something similar can be said of music; one indication of an interesting work or performance is that while we enjoy what we hear, we also want to know what will happen next. So music that we find absorbing both dominates our thoughts in the moment and keeps us engaged for longer.

A second feature of music that makes it particularly well suited to providing an intense focus is its lack of clear verbal meaning. This extends even to songs and holds true even when - and this is frequently not the case - the words are fully comprehensible. The meaning of a song, like that of a poem, is not reducible to the meaning of the words of which it is composed. The indeterminacy of music's meaning ensures that it remains "open" to listeners. This is not to say that any musical passage might have any meaning. There are constraints on what meanings can in general be expressed by music, and on what meanings can be read from particular works. But to a large extent, listeners can hear in music what they need to hear. Or the burdens of interpretation can be set aside and listeners need recover no particular meaning at all.

These qualities of music - its unfolding narrative structure and its lack of determinate meaning - make it very well suited to providing an object of sustained focus. Such a focus can take one out of oneself; this happens when internal speech is silenced and replaced by music. The work of self-management is temporarily set aside. When the music ceases and this work is picked up again, the benefits of such an intense external focus remain.

7

THE SUBLIME, REVISITED

In certain passages it evokes sobs and I feel totally crushed - my listening is fully concentrated, and the rest of the world disappears in a way, and I become merged in the music or the music in me, it fills me completely. I also get physical reactions...wet eyes, a breathing that gets sobbing in certain passages, a feeling of crying in my throat and chest. Trying to find words for the emotions themselves, I would like to use words as: crushed, shaken, tragedy, maybe death, absorption, but also tenderness, longing, desire (vain), a will to live, prayer. The whole experience also has the character of a total standstill, a kind of meditative rest, a last definite and absolute end, after which nothing else can follow.

Unnamed volunteer, report to the SEM Project

A lofty passage does not convince the reason of the reader, but takes him out of himself. That which is admirable ever confounds our judgement, and eclipses that which is merely reasonable or agreeable. To believe or not is usually in our own power; but the Sublime, acting with an imperious and irresistible force, sways every reader whether he will or no.

Longinus, *On the Sublime* (i)

that which excites in us, without any reasoning about it, but in the mere apprehension of it, the feeling of the sublime may appear, as regards its form, to violate purpose in respect of the judgment, to be unsuited to our presentative faculty, and as it were to do violence to the imagination; and yet it is judged to be only the more sublime. (§23)

For just as we charge with want of *taste* the man who is indifferent when passing judgment upon an object of nature that we regard as beautiful, so we say of him who remains unmoved in the presence of that which we judge to be sublime: He has no *feeling*. (§29)

Kant, *Critique of Judgement*

Throughout this book we have been trying to make sense of responses to music like the one recounted by the unnamed volunteer in the first epigraph to this chapter. I have described these as "strong emotional" and as "sublime" responses, thereby placing them in a philosophical tradition extending from Longinus to Kant and beyond. In doing so, I have used "sublime" in a way that, while not opposed to traditional usage, does not fully cohere with it either. Steering clear of value judgements and ontological commitments, I have remained neutral as to whether the musical works that seem to arouse such responses were themselves "really" sublime or not. In this chapter we face these more normative issues squarely. What is the relationship between the sublime and beauty, and between the sublime and artistic greatness? How are feelings of the sublime related to other possible types of responses to music? What is gained and what is lost in treating sublime responses as fundamentally emotional in nature?

There is no way to be certain whether the emotions reported by volunteers to the SEM project, or the chills experienced by subjects in various experimental studies, or the tears recalled by those who responded to psychologists' questionnaires, represent bona fide experiences of the sublime. We do not have a systematic or comprehensive "theory of the sublime" that we can use to test such responses or to guide experimental work. No single region of the brain "lights up" in the presence of a truly sublime stimulus, and the equivalent of a polygraph test to assess the sublimity of listeners' responses to music does not exist. (Nor are polygraph tests completely reliable!) The sublime is a philosophical concept that emerges at a distinct point in history, gains prominence at a later point and is eclipsed by other concepts still later. The concept of the sublime changes with different thinkers, each of whom interprets it within a different conceptual framework and emphasizes different features. Yet a few key characteristics retain their importance throughout this history. One such enduring feature is the conviction that sublime objects and the responses they provoke subvert reason. They get under our defences and take us out of ourselves. The sublime, in whatever form it is found, challenges our mental powers without overwhelming them. These are the same features that I have found to be so prominent in the listeners' descriptions of responses to the music that moves them.

Placing what are somewhat dryly called "strong" responses to music within the tradition of the philosophical sublime is fruitful for a number of reasons. Although the concept of the sublime has a definite history and cultural background, the qualities it embodies resonate in other cultural traditions. By examining a great variety of such responses under the same rubric, we can see their commonalities. A teenager dancing to techno-music at a rave in Toronto feels a sense of boundaries dissolving, and kinship and unity with those around him. A worshipper in a Pentecostal church in Boston sings along with the choir and feels taken out of herself and connected with something greater. Are the feelings and internal experiences of these two really so different? Does music play a similar role in both? If so, what is it about music that allows it to play such a role? Treating both types of responses as at least potentially sublime allows us to ask these questions and, perhaps, to begin to answer them.

There is one major difference between the way "sublime" has been used in this book and the way it has been understood in the philosophical tradition. Longinus, Kant and others considered "sublime" a term of high, if sometimes nervous, praise. Sublime objects - whether vast, craggy mountains, statues or rhetorical passages - are special. They command our attention even as they sometimes confound it. Yet throughout the tradition, "sublime" refers to such special and distinctive objects, as well as to the responses of those who encounter them. For Kant, remember, it is ultimately the human mind that is sublime, not any of the objects that give rise to the feeling of the sublime. I have examined responses to music that seemed to me "sublime" without bothering too much about whether the music that inspired them was "really" sublime and worthy of such responses or not. Certainly, some of the musical works mentioned in the previous chapters are among the greatest ever composed; others do not merit such high praise. Just what are the connections between the sublime, artistic value, taste and morality?

BEAUTY, THE SUBLIME AND STRONG EMOTIONS

> The intense feelings which music awakens in us and all the moods, painful as well as delightful, into which it lulls us as we daydream: these we by no means wish to minimize. Indeed, it belongs to the most beautiful and redeeming mysteries that, by grace of God, art is able to call forth such otherworldly stirrings in us. It is only against unscientific exploitation of these facts as aesthetical principles that we lodge our complaint.
>
> Eduard Hanslick, *On the Musically Beautiful*

Can something be both sublime and beautiful? Edmund Burke, one of the most influential writers on the sublime, insisted on a complete disjunction between the beautiful and the sublime. Beauty is founded on pleasure, and the sublime on pain. Burke has sometimes been taken to mean that sublime objects could not also be beautiful, and vice versa. But this is not exactly what he said, and indeed, any such understanding of the sublime which posits it in strict opposition to beauty seems wrong-headed. According to Burke, beauty and sublimity could indeed be found in a single object, but each of these qualities would have to be explained differently. It seems clear that to separate beauty and sublimity too forcefully - as if the presence of one would always crowd out the other - is to risk being uninformative, both about the experience of the sublime and about the objects which inspire sublime responses. We have seen that central to the idea of the sublime is its appeal to emotion and its power to circumvent reason. In the words of Longinus, sublime passages take the reader out of himself. Some of the things which have such an effect, although they may inspire terror and awe, are also beautiful. Historically, there has been support among philosophers for the idea that a very high degree of beauty is also sublime. When we consider some of the things which have been thought to be sublime - mountains, rainbows, storms at sea, hurricanes, the pyramids - it would seem that nothing is lost in thinking that they may be both sublime *and* beautiful. There is another problem with maintaining a strict disjunction between the sublime and the beautiful: our concept of the beautiful is diminished. To say that an object that is attractive yet also somehow troubling or eerie is sublime but not also beautiful is seriously to deplete the idea of the beautiful. A robust idea of beauty, as distinct from mere prettiness or cuteness, must be allowed to encompass such "ambivalent" objects.

But if the sublime is best understood as at least sometimes overlapping with the beautiful, as seems correct, then is there still a need for it as a separate concept? Perhaps "the sublime" is an old-fashioned and otiose idea, an abstraction we might be better to do without. Here I think we are better off resisting the impulse to wield Occam's razor. Although they overlap, the beautiful and the sublime are not coextensive. Again, it depends on how restrictive a notion of beauty we are willing to support. Ordinary usage of "beautiful" and its synonyms ("attractive," "lovely," "good-looking," "handsome," and so on) would seem to support a fairly wide application, alongside a separate higher class of the "truly" or "very" beautiful ("exquisite," "gorgeous"). For example, on the street where I live a number of people are keen and accomplished gardeners. Anytime between May and September you can see several very fine gardens - featuring well-kept lawns bordered with colourful flowers, carefully arranged rocks and greenery, tastefully chosen ornamental sculpture, trellises with climbing vines, majestic trees, and so on. The term "beautiful" seems appropriate to describe a number of my neighbours' gardens. Yet one July in one of those gardens a gigantic, orange-red, sunburst-coloured iris bloomed, which was, I would have to say, extremely beautiful. The garden was on one of my regular routes and I sometimes passed it several times in a day. Each time I would have to stop and admire the iris. I saw others doing the same, sometimes coming over from the other side of the street to get a better look. If we allow that beauty admits of degrees and that sublimity can sometimes consist in a very high degree of beauty, then the iris has a claim to being both beautiful and sublime.

It is challenging but not impossible to think of music that is sublime without also being beautiful. Readers may have their own examples. I find some Blues and old folk recordings to be sublime but not beautiful, in particular, Reverend Gary Davis's take on "Death Don't Have No Mercy." And several years ago, as part of a museum exhibit, I heard and have not forgotten a recording of some old Shaker women singing the Shaker hymn "Simple Gifts" with moving simplicity and dignity. Certainly, most of the music we have considered in the previous chapters has been both sublime and beautiful if it has been either. Yet the reverse does not hold: many beautiful works are not sublime and many ways of responding to the beautiful in music do not constitute strong emotional responses. Beautiful music can be delightful, glorious, charming or amusing rather than awesome. One can be quietly appreciative rather than crushed, or touched rather than overwhelmed by the beauty of music. It is useful to have terms for both kinds of (mainly positive) responses, and we need the concept of the sublime to describe those responses to music and art (and the works that inspire them) that are very intense and go beyond everyday reactions. It is a term we can use when "beauty" is not strong enough, or the beauty in question is too complicated or ambivalent to resist further comment.

Earlier I said that explanations of strong emotional responses to music along the lines of "I cried because the music was so beautiful" would have to be eschewed. Such "explanations" are not illuminating because they replace one mystery (the response to music) with another (the response to beauty). But the person who says, "I cried because the music was beautiful," may have something else in mind. She may not be offering an explanation, so much as claiming that no explanation is *possible*. She may be saying, in effect, "We have hit bedrock. Explanations can go no further." But do we have to accept this? Must explanations really come to an end at some point? While it may be the case that our powers of explanation have definite limits, we cannot decide where those limits are and curtail our inquiries at the outset. My explanation of strong emotional responses to music may not in the end be satisfactory, but it does not follow that no explanation is possible.

Clearly beauty ("aesthetic value" if you prefer) has some connection with sublime responses. Many works which prompt strong emotional responses to music are critically acclaimed, and some are considered to be among the greatest in their respective genres. What contribution does beauty make to strong emotional experiences of music? Do all beautiful works arouse strong responses in suitably prepared and educated listeners? Do strong responses reliably indicate great works of music? The music critic Eduard Hanslick was strongly opposed to the idea that a musical work's power to arouse feelings in listeners was indicative of its artistic worth. He did not deny that music could arouse such feelings; however, such feelings did not "count" towards a work's merit, but said more about the listeners who experienced them than they did about the work that inspired them.

There is surely something to what Hanslick says. Personal associations can play a large role in our responses to musical works and in our assessment of them. A listener who is often deeply moved by music is not necessarily a good judge of that music's merit. A cool demeanour may mask great insight into music and a profound appreciation of it. However, we would be naïve to discount the power of music's beauty. Beautiful things, especially extremely beautiful things, can have very strong effects on us. They "grab" us, whether we expect it or not. The philosopher Guy Sircello described this phenomenon very well: "We don't, generally speaking, simply see, feel, hear, taste, or otherwise apprehend beauty. Beauty is typically an attention-getter; we suddenly notice it; it breaks into our consciousness. Moreover, it does so gratuitously; it does so despite the fact that we may not have been looking for it, despite the fact that we had no inkling it was going to be there." This conveys almost exactly the effect that my neighbour's beautiful iris had on me and others. Its extreme beauty stood out among all of the less spectacularly beautiful flowers on the street. I simply felt I had no choice but to stop and admire it. Furthermore, very beautiful things not only grab our attention, they also have a powerful hold over us. Sircello again: "When we perceive a beautiful thing, we don't want to let it go, we never want to stop perceiving it. It is as if our eyes wanted to drown in the sight, our ears in the sound. When the beautiful thing has disappeared, or when we have gone our way, we sense a loss, we feel let down." This sense of loss - an intimation of mortality, of one day all things coming to an end - is perhaps the source of the pain that many commentators have argued is an aspect of the feeling of the sublime. Extremely and unambiguously beautiful objects may not be frightening, but the reality of their transitory nature can be sobering, if not painful.

The "stickiness" of beauty - its ability to impinge on our consciousness and absorb it for a time - seems to be at work in some cases of strong emotional responses to music. The listener's attention is seized and then held by the beauty of the music. He has no choice but to listen. If the music were not so beautiful, the listener would not have to devote his full attention to it, but could continue in his previous activity, perhaps listening with "half an ear." When a listener is fully engaged in listening, the music can work as a stimulus at the neurological level and can also be understood as an object of cognition, making for a richer experience.

SUBLIME/BEAUTIFUL/PROFOUND

The sublime in music also needs to be distinguished from the profound. Other thinkers have treated as examples of the "profound" the same types of experiences that I have called sublime. What is profundity in music, and how is it different from the sublime? Could we get along without either of these concepts, or do we need both? Like many listeners, I have had the sensation that the music I was listening to was "profound," in the way that a poem or even a single remark might be profound. The key thing here - and the source of the philosophical difficulty - is that profundity is linked with knowledge. We speak of "profound" scientific discoveries; a profound remark is insightful or wise. A profound literary work is one that can bring home to us truths that we may already know but have failed to keep in mind. Tolstoy's novella *The Death of Ivan Ilych* is profound in a number of ways. It has a profound content in the moral teachings it conveys - the certainty of death and the importance of compassion. Even more profound is the way in which it is able forcibly to remind the reader of the significance of those teachings. Tolstoy's novella is also profoundly moving or distressing to readers, in the sense of deeply or strongly affecting. *The Death of Ivan Ilych* is both profound and profoundly moving. There would seem to be no reason why something could not be (cognitively) profound without being also profoundly (deeply) moving.

The philosophical difficulty about the profundity of music has to do with this first (adjectival) meaning of the word. Of course, music can be deeply - profoundly - moving: who would argue otherwise? The problem arises when we ask whether music can be profound in the sense that is connected with knowledge. So we would do well to keep the problem of musical profundity separate from questions about the emotional power and effects of music, which are more appropriately and fruitfully classed with the musical sublime. Furthermore, we have seen that some of the musical works that seem most able to move listeners profoundly (deeply) are not ones that anybody would likely be tempted to call profound in the sense of conveying insight. The chill-inducing "I Will Always Love You," with its fairly banal lyrics, is a case in point.

Is any music "profound" in the same sense that Tolstoy's *The Death of Ivan Ilych* is profound? The philosopher Peter Kivy prompted a storm of criticism when he argued in his book *Music Alone* that there was no rational justification for saying that instrumental music was profound. Taking profound literature as a paradigm, Kivy characterized profound works of art as those which both have a profound subject matter and treat that subject matter in a way adequate to its profundity. That is, profound works of art are those that say profound things about a profound subject matter at a very high level of artistic or aesthetic excellence. Since instrumental music cannot "say" anything, it cannot be "about" anything, let alone about anything profound. So, instrumental music cannot be profound. Kivy's critics fell roughly into two groups. Some took issue with the literary or verbal character of "aboutness" that Kivy employed. For example, a string quartet could invoke or bring to mind the human condition and so be about it. That may be different from the way in which a literary work is about the human condition, but then music is not literature. Other critics challenged Kivy's notion of profundity and explored the subjective, internal experience of listeners who claimed to find music profound.

Perhaps less well noticed and discussed than Kivy's arguments in *Music Alone* was his avowal that he was unable to restrain himself from calling certain works profound:

> And in spite of the fact that there seems to me to be substantial agreement among enthusiasts about which musical works deserve the description "profound," I fail to see any rational justification for their deserving it. Yet, for certain works, I can find no other word as appropriate. Yes: the *Well-Tempered Clavier* and the late Beethoven quartets are great works of art. So also are Mozart's divertimenti for winds. But the former are something else, they are profound, and there's an end on it.

It would seem that Kivy has not changed his mind. In a later article he admits parenthetically: "I have been known to describe the *Eroica* as a 'profound human utterance', although I do not think it is either an utterance or profound." Why does Kivy - who has provided such compelling arguments for the view that music *cannot* be profound - nonetheless persist in saying otherwise? I believe that there is something else going on here besides the philosopher's urge to "think with the learned and speak with the vulgar." One might just as well ask why so many of Kivy's colleagues in philosophical aesthetics sought to refute him, and why so many other intelligent people who know music well persist in their belief that music can be profound. I will quote only one example. The great music theorist Leonard Meyer linked our emotional responses to music with the expectations aroused by a work's structure and argued for an account of value in music that drew heavily on information theory. But when it came to distinguishing good from great music he pointed to something else: "And the greatest works would be those which embody value of the highest order with the most profound - and I use the word without hesitation - content."

Of course, general consensus, even unanimity, does not make a claim true, but if ascribing profundity to music is a mistake, why is it such a long-lived and persistent one, made by people who perhaps should know better? Kivy suggests that when we call music profound we are invoking a "courtesy" definition, as when, for example, we say that the pastry chef's latest creation is "a work of art," even when we know that it is no such thing. But this suggestion will not get us very far. Perhaps the pastry chef is a latterday Marie-Antoine Carême (the eighteenth-century master of *haute cuisine*), who will challenge our conception of what constitutes an artwork so that we do in fact want to say that his creation is a bona fide artwork. And if "profound" is extended to music only out of courtesy, then why that particular term of praise? Had Kivy argued that music could not be "mouth-watering" or "scrumptious" I doubt he would have provoked the response that he did. Music is not routinely described in terms more appropriate for food, but there is a tradition of calling some musical works profound. Why should this be? And if it is due to a confusion of the attributes and values of music with those of literature, then why is this particular confusion so enduring?

It seems to me that our propensity to say that music is profound - even to defend this view in the face of the feeling that we should perhaps know better - is significant. To return to our original question: Is any music profound, in the sense of being connected with knowledge, in the same sense that *The Death of Ivan Ilych* is profound? Probably not; but then, Tolstoy's novella is not profound in the same way that Einstein's theory of relativity or Darwin's theory of evolution by means of natural selection is profound, and neither of these is profound in the same way that the solution to an intractable mathematical problem is profound. Yet "profound" seems the right term for all of them, even if we cannot say exactly what it is they have in common. "Profound" is not univocal; it carries different nuances and significations in different contexts. One of these contexts is our appreciation of certain musical works. So Kivy was correct in praising the *Well-Tempered Clavier* and the late Beethoven quartets as profound. His arguments only go to show that the term "profound" is legitimately used in a variety of ways.

MUSIC AND MORALITY

A long intellectual tradition - from the ancient Greeks to contemporary critics of hiphop - insists on the connection between music and morality. Morality is an abiding theme of musical discourse. Composers, performers, critics and listeners have always discussed music in moral terms. What is behind such talk? How does it relate to the value of music - both the value of particular works and of music in general? Where does the musical sublime figure in such discussions? Two British philosophers, Colin Radford and Roger Scruton, have addressed these issues. Both seem to accept variations of the position advocated by Socrates in the *Republic*. Accordingly, music expresses - and may in turn elicit - certain emotions and responses, all of which are proper objects of moral judgement.

Radford's claims are the more modest. In the article 'How Can Music Be Moral?' he asks how a "mere sequence of sounds" can be moral. His main concern is with "what is inherent in the music" and so he concentrates on "absolute" or non-programmatic music as opposed to music with words. Rather than answer his question regarding the morality of sounds directly, Radford narrows his enquiry to focus on another, no less difficult question. He sets out to "explain and justify" his intuition that the music of Mozart is superior to that of Tchaikovsky - not simply superior as music, but *morally* superior as well. Here is his description of the music of Mozart:

> [A] Mozart violin concerto, e.g., his third, might begin with a first movement the beauty of the melody, the tempo, orchestration, and development of which is not only beautiful but exhilarating. Indeed it may feel as if, and be, that this particular beauty is not sad, that is, sadness is somehow and almost entirely denied, i.e., not indulged. This is followed by a slow, poignant movement, in which, again, the feeling - this time of aching sadness - is somehow resolved at the end of the movement. This composition is then completed by something predominantly gay, brilliant, and emotionally, almost, "lightweight."

And again:

> But what has [Mozart] to be sad about? More particularly, what sadness is his Quintet in G Minor an expression of? Mozart is aware of and gives expression to a sadness that is global as it can

be, sadness at life, at being human. As we have already noticed, we have to say this if we allow ourselves to say anything. And he is aware of it, but does not indulge it. Not to be aware of it is to be shallow [....] He was aware of this feeling, and so felt it, and yet he did not indulge it.

Radford finds dignity and restraint in Mozart's music. In contrast,

Well, consider almost any composition by Tchaikowsky. So lyr-ical, beautiful, sad, yearning - and for me, too yearning. This is music in which sadness is indulged and which indulges sadness. [...] Tchaikowsky's work is sentimental and that is a moral fault! Either he is blind to its sentimentality or corruptly indulges it.

Radford's characterization of Mozart's music seems just. Indeed, he has identified and articulated the "smiling through tears" quality which is so evocative and moving in the best performances of some of Mozart's music and yet so difficult to capture in words. But it remains to be seen whether these features of Mozart's work are most effectively brought out in comparison with the music of Tchaikovsky. The com-parison yields little insight into the specific qualities and strengths of either composer. Too much separates them: nationality, temperament, historical and cultural context, style. It would have been more enlight-ening to compare Mozart with, say, his contemporary Austrian com-poser Johannes Hummel and Tchaikovsky with, say, his contemporary Russian composer Modest Mussorgsky.

Leaving aside the appropriateness of the comparison, how judicious is Radford's assessment of Tchaikovsky? It is interesting to note that, although Radford tells us that he will consider performances rather than compositions in his article, he does not mention a specific performance of any work of either composer. We may agree that some of the least sen-sitive performances of Tchaikovsky's least impressive compositions may indeed seem overwrought. Yet, on the whole, Radford's assessment does not strike me as well founded; to my ear at least, sadness is not indulged in "almost any" composition by Tchaikovsky. Let us, for the sake of argument, assume that Radford is correct in his assessment of both

Mozart and Tchaikovsky, and that it actually is the case that Mozart's music manifests dignity and restraint, while Tchaikovsky's is sentimental and indulges in sadness. Is Radford's intuition that Mozart's music is thereby morally superior to Tchaikovsky's validated? It would be, if you think that restraint is appropriate to every situation and that there is necessarily something wrong with "indulging" or yielding to negative emotion. These suggestions seem to me to be far from obvious.

While Radford is convinced that music, and our responses to it, can have a moral dimension, he does not make the stronger claim that music invariably affects character. He accepts the possibility, exemplified by some Nazis, that a person might respond with delight to music which manifests moral awareness, yet still be wicked. Moral awareness in music is an indispensable condition, but one "which guarantees nothing." There is no necessary relationship between taste and the capacity for virtue. Scruton, by contrast, does not shrink from making claims about the links between aesthetic and moral judgement, between good taste and the capacity for virtue. Indeed, he sees the search for objective musical values as one part of a search for the right way to live. As I read him, Scruton offers two related arguments for this position; the first can be called the "sentimental education" argument, and the second the "mimesis" argument.

Both arguments rely on Scruton's thought-provoking and original account of involvement with music. According to him, the response to expression in music is a sympathetic response, awakened by another life or subjectivity. A sympathetic response occurs when we come to share another's joy, anger, and so on, without feeling it for ourselves. Since, on Scruton's account, music does not have the capacity to represent, the life to which we respond in music is abstract and indeterminate - there is no precise object of our sympathy. In addition to feelings, actions and gestures may also be sympathetic, and, like sympathetic feelings, sympathetic gestures may arise in response to real or aesthetic contexts. Scruton understands dancing as potentially sympathetic in this way:

> In dancing I respond to another's gestures, move with him, or in harmony with him, without seeking to change his predicament

or share his burden. [... Dancing] involves responding to movement for its own sake, dwelling in the appearance of another's
gesture, finding meaning in that appearance, and matching it
with a gesture of my own.

Silent listening can also be a kind of dancing: "Our whole being is
absorbed by the movement of the music, and moves with it, compelled
by incipient gestures of imitation." The response of the listener, then, is
a sublimated desire to "move with" the music. One of the reasons why
it *matters* what type of music we choose to listen to is that through this
sympathetic response our emotions can become educated, but at the
same time corrupted.

Scruton's 'sentimental education' argument for the connections
between aesthetic and moral judgement begins by claiming that works
of art can fail in two ways: they can fail to interest us; or they can invite
an interest of which we disapprove. While he cites pornography and
gratuitous violence as examples of the latter, his comments on poetry
show that "an interest of which we disapprove" is meant to be construed quite broadly:

A poem is describing or invoking something; it is also taking up
an attitude. A wrong word is not just one that sounds wrong, but
one that reveals some failure to observe, some insensitivity to
the experience conveyed, some emotional ignorance or coldness.
We should not be surprised by this: after all, it happens in life
too - one word may show that someone is professing a love, or
sympathy that he does not feel, or which he finds appropriate for
some self-dramatizing purpose. Reading poetry is a way in which
we become sensitive to this, and so understand how and when to
extend our sympathies.

Scruton's discussion of the moral qualities of music parallels these
remarks on poetry. We can recognize the way in which our sympathies
are enlisted by a piece of music - tired rhetorical gestures, stock devices
or an inflation of effect not appropriate to the subject matter - and con-
done or recoil from it as we see fit. Our judgement of taste in reading

poetry is the same as that which governs our choice of friends, and our judgement of taste in music is no different from our judgement of taste in poetry. It follows that our ability to discern what is appropriate or fitting in musical works is of a piece with our capability to detect insincerity and pretence in people.

One example Scruton gives of music which inappropriately enlists our sympathies is the well-known (and to many people very moving) aria "Un bel dì vedremo" from Puccini's *Madam Butterfly*. He is critical of both the text of the aria and of the music to which Puccini sets it. However, Scruton's analysis of the aria raises some questions. First, his account of how we can recognize that our sympathies may be inappropriately enlisted by "Un bel dì vedremo" assumes a high degree of musical and cultural literacy. It is one thing not to like the aria but not be able to say why, and another thing to be able to give an account of how one's sympathies are being enlisted by the composer or performers. For example, how many listeners could say, with Scruton, "Moving in one stride out of G flat major into B flat minor, [Puccini] mobilizes the orchestra around a subdominant cadence, using the major triad for rhetorical effect, so as to break decisively through the barrier of G flat on to G natural, before stepping as suddenly back again." As Scruton nowhere indicates that he wants to restrict good taste to those trained in musicology, his insistence that good taste requires recognizing the "precise way" our sympathies are enlisted by music is puzzling.

However, let us agree for the sake of argument that Scruton's analysis of the aria is correct, and assume that he does not mean his model of musical competence to exclude most listeners. Some difficulties nonetheless remain. Scruton's argument begs the question by assuming that sensitivity to emotion in music, developed in aesthetic contexts, entails sensitivity to emotion in people, in non-aesthetic contexts. Yet knowledge of how music works and enlists our sympathies does not necessarily entail knowledge of how human beings enlist our sympathies, inappropriately or not. If it did, the greatest composers and performers would be gifted psychologists, even when they turned their attention from composing or stepped away from the concert stage, and I know of no evidence that this is in fact the case. Furthermore, Scruton has not shown that Puccini's purported failure in the aria is to invite an interest of which we disapprove, rather than simply a failure to inter-est. It is not obvious that an interest in overwrought emotion is invari-ably to be condemned.

Scruton's "mimesis" argument likewise relies on his account of involvement with music as a type of latent dancing. Scruton makes a connection between the social aspects of dancing and the gestures and movements of social life more generally. Manners, for instance, are said to be a kind of generalized choreography. Plato's conviction that dancing is a reflection of social character is "surely right," and by social character Scruton understands a way of life, habits of mind and character, and ways of responding to one another in the circum-stances of social life. It is this link between music and social life which prompts Scruton to call music a "character forming force" and lament the decline of taste in popular music. In his own words: "Listen to a gavotte from the late Renaissance, and imagine the mores of the people who danced to it. Then listen to a track by Nirvana and imagine the mores of the people who can dance to *that*."

Even if we allow Scruton his point and agree that dance is a reflec-tion of social character, it remains to be seen that today's popular music and the dancing inspired by it are morally inferior to the music and dance of the late Renaissance. The grace and composure exemplified by a gavotte may reflect that era's religious and social intolerance, just as a track by Nirvana may well reflect today's more democratic values and disdain for social prejudice. And even if we agree with Scruton that the aesthetic taste expressed by Nirvana fans is lamentable, it still remains to be seen that their lack of taste reflects a diminished moral sense. Neither a developed capacity for the feelings of others nor the "correct" social values can guarantee the only thing arguably essential for moral virtue - the presence of good will.

Can we draw any conclusions about moral judgements of music from this brief examination of Scruton and Radford? It would seem that both philosophers err in focusing their discussion on the appro-priateness of certain emotions in music, whether or not they make the stronger claim that these emotions influence listeners. The line between moral and non-moral music cannot be drawn simply on the basis of which emotions music expresses, nor on how the emotions are expressed (with or without "appropriate" restraint, for example). This is because in our non-musical lives the line between morally appropriate and inappropriate emotional responses cannot be drawn with clarity or distinction. The presence of "sentimentality" in music may be an aesthetic demerit, but neither Scruton nor Radford shows that it is also a moral failing.

How, then, to make judgements of the moral worth of different musical works, composers or genres? On that subject it is perhaps better to say too little rather than too much. It seems important to distinguish between the claims of taste, aesthetic judgements and moral judgements, in order to avoid the tendency to moralize aesthetics and condemn the musical works one dislikes on moral as well as aesthetic grounds. I would say that in the absence of a title or other clear evidence of the composer's intentions, we cannot *fault* music for lacking moral awareness. In other words, we are entitled to judge that work in terms of its moral awareness only if we are reasonably sure that the composer meant to evoke a response to a certain subject, and that the subject is a proper locus of *moral* response. In the absence of evidence that Mozart meant to communicate something about our emotional lives, any moral awareness we might hear in his music is a bonus. Similarly, in the absence of evidence that Tchaikovsky meant to evoke a moral response in his music, our lack of such response is *not* an aesthetic demerit. Put another way, the only clear case in which we can condemn a lack of moral awareness in music is when we are reasonably certain that the composer intended the music to be a response to a subject worthy of moral response. So a musical work that has no clear subject or whose subject is not properly moral does not attempt to elicit a moral response and cannot be faulted because it does not. A composition on a subject worthy of moral response - say, war, tragic death or natural disasters such as the eighteenth-century Lisbon earthquake - is properly judged as aesthetically inferior if it does not evoke a moral response.

Radford's conviction that some music, most notably Mozart's, articulates and displays "moral awareness" does strike me as true. Although Radford does not give anything like a definition of this quality, I have an idea of what he means because I feel that I have heard this quality myself. But what, if anything, does this feeling rest on? What does it amount to? Perhaps this: music that displays moral awareness brings about a certain type of reaction in the listener, which we might call a "sit up and listen" reaction. This is first and foremost a response to qualities inherent in the music as heard. Of course, there are many reasons why we may "sit up and listen" to music: a performance may strike us as particularly fine or particularly bad; the music in question may be unfamiliar or carry personal associations; we may be unsure whether we recognize a work and attend to it in hope of making an identification. There are at least two ways in which such a "sit up and listen" reaction might be characterized as a response to the music's moral awareness - an easy way and a difficult way.

The most obvious reason listeners might "hear" moral awareness is that they hear the music as a response to a subject worthy of moral concern. They would most likely do so because of their knowledge of the work's title, composer or the circumstances surrounding its composition. The knowledge that one is listening to a requiem or threnody or a composition dedicated to a particular individual can shape our response to it. But readers might recall that Radford limited his discussion of morality in music to absolute music, without a descriptive title or programme, so as better to bring out the philosophical issue at hand: Can a "mere sequence of sounds" be moral? While I admire Radford's insistence on making the philosophical problem to be considered as difficult as possible, I am nonetheless convinced that his approach is misguided. The answer to the question "Can a mere sequence of sounds be moral?" is a resounding no. But music is *not* a "mere sequence of sounds," and I doubt that most listeners respond to it as such. Radford has underestimated the cultural and historical situatedness of musical composers, performers and listeners. Music, even so-called absolute music, is composed, performed and listened to in a specific context, and so to treat music as sound, pure and simple, is misguided.

There is a second, more difficult way in which music might bring about a "sit up and listen" reaction. The moral awareness of absolute music is to be located in the ways in which it makes a listener aware of her capacity for empathy and emotional response, and aware of the possible limits of that capacity. Certain works of music, especially when performed with great skill and sensitivity, can make a listener suspect

that the depth or quality of emotion expressed is deeper or more poignant than any feeling with which she had previously been familiar. Such
a listener recognizes the expressive qualities in the music she hears and
is *challenged* by them. That is, she comes to suspect that her capacity
for empathy is called into question by the emotions expressed in the
music. The music expresses, say, a depth of sorrow she had not previously encountered, and she is unsure how to respond. In such cases,
the listener is not necessarily aware why she responds to the music as
she does. An analogy with Kant's analysis of judgements of the sublime
seems appropriate here. As we saw earlier, that which gives rise to a
judgement of the sublime - the raging sea, a violent thunderstorm or the
vast scale of the pyramids - is not, strictly speaking, the object of the
judgement. Rather, in contemplating such phenomena, the feeling of
the sublime is aroused by the failure of the imagination to comprehend
great magnitude. The object of judgements of the sublime turns out to
be the realization that a part of one is "super-sensible" - not subject to
the laws of nature and thus potentially autonomous. Similarly, when
a listener makes a judgement that a particular work of absolute music
displays moral awareness, the object of the judgement is not, strictly
speaking, the music itself, but the feelings aroused in the listener by the
music. Thus listeners who respond to the moral awareness in Mozart's
third violin concerto are responding to the expressive qualities which
Radford identifies, namely, aching sadness, which is somehow resolved.
These qualities prompt some listeners to "sit up and listen" because, at
some level, the successful resolution of sadness which Mozart conveys
challenges their own capacity to put aside negative emotion.

One of the merits of my account of moral awareness in music is that
the feelings which I identify at its core - awareness of a capacity for
emotional response and of the possible inadequacy of that capacity -
may be aroused by music *even if* the listener rarely exercises a capacity
for emotion. That is, my analysis does not require that a "sit up and
listen" response to music's moral awareness prompts listeners to morally informed behaviour or even to greater insight into their emotional
lives. Like the music-loving Nazis mentioned by Radford, a person
who responds to music which manifests moral awareness in the way I
have suggested can still be wicked.

For music to display moral awareness, then, it must be of a very high aesthetic quality relative to other works in the same genre. In making moral awareness supervenient upon aesthetic worth in some cases have I not merely redefined moral awareness as the (arguably) less elusive attribute of aesthetic worth? No. To draw on an insight from Scruton's position, art can fail in two ways: it can invite an interest of which we disapprove, or it can fail to interest us. If music fails to interest, it simply cannot bring about the types of reaction I have been describing. Thus it turns out to be no coincidence that the work of minor composers is rarely held up as illustrative of music's moral value.

We value music for many different reasons - aesthetic, emotional, intellectual, practical, even moral. The concept of the sublime has a role to play in our appreciation of music. It can be used as a term of high praise for the greatest, profoundest and most moving music that we know. It can also name those musical and emotional experiences of music that go beyond standard or customary experiences, if we are fortunate enough to have them.

CONCLUSION: VALUES

AN EXPERIMENT

It was the most astonishing thing I've ever seen in Washington. Joshua Bell was standing there playing at rush hour, and people were not stopping, and not even looking, and some were flipping quarters at him! Quarters! I wouldn't do that to anybody. I was thinking, *Omigosh, what kind of a city do I live in that this could happen?*

Stacy Furukawa, quoted in *The Washington Post*

In early 2007, a staff writer at *The Washington Post* organized an unscientific but revealing experiment. What would happen if a world-class musician performed incognito in the Washington Metro during the morning rush hour? Would he be recognized? Would commuters stop and listen? Would they give him any money? The paper approached Joshua Bell, acknowledged to be one of the finest violinists in the world, and owner of one of the finest violins in the world - a Stradivarius crafted in 1713. Bell agreed and, dressed in casual clothes and a baseball cap, he treated commuters at L'Enfant Plaza Station in the heart of Washington to a free concert. The pieces he played were among the greatest musical works ever written, including the famous Bach "Chaconne" from the *Partita No. 2 in D minor* - surely a sublime musical work if any is. Editors at the paper thought there might be a problem with crowd control if Bell was recognized, and certainly in such a sophisticated demographic as Washington this was a strong possibility. What if so many people gathered that rush-hour pedestrian traffic backed up and tempers flared? They discussed how to deal with possible outcomes. The experiment was conceived as a test of context, perception, priorities and public taste. As they put it: "In a banal setting at an inconvenient time, would beauty transcend?"

The answer, sadly, was no. Bell performed for 43 minutes, secretly videotaped by the *Post*. Over a thousand people walked by Bell; only seven stopped to listen for at least a minute. Twenty-seven people gave money, but most of them rushed by. In all, donations came to about $32. There was no crowd, and only one person recognized Bell, towards the end of his performance. (This was Stacy Furukawa, quoted above.) Most of the people who walked past and were caught on video seemed utterly oblivious and absorbed in their daily pursuits: getting to work on time, buying a lottery ticket or newspaper, sipping coffee. A few weeks after the *Post* published its article on the experiment, the British newspaper the *Independent*, perhaps hopeful that British musical discrimination would prove superior to American, repeated the experiment in London. Tasmin Little, another world-class violinist fortunate enough to own a Stradivarius, performed for passers-by in the railway bridge next to Waterloo Station. She also played Bach's "Chaconne" and a number of other works, with similar dismal results as the American experiment. Little was recognized a few times. But out of the 900-1000 people who walked by, only eight stopped to listen and donations came to just over £14.

Why, in both cases, did so few people stop? One factor that cannot be discounted is time pressure. Many of those who passed by likely had trains to catch or appointments to keep. Others, preoccupied by cell phone conversations or listening on headphones to music they had chosen themselves or to audio books, may simply not have noticed the musicians. Throughout this book I have been asking why music moves us. How is it that a sequence of sounds with no clear verbal meaning can cause feelings of awe, as well as physical symptoms like tears and chills in listeners? The results of these experiments represent, in a sense, the inverse of the questions I have been considering. Why would great music expertly performed *fail* to move listeners? Why might such music not even be noticed? I will return to these questions at the end of the chapter.

VALUE AND THE SUBLIME IN MUSIC

Is music that can arouse experiences of sublime better or more valuable than music that does not? We have to be careful about what we mean by "value" here. According to one definition value is largely subjective. A photograph has "sentimental value" for me if it holds some significance for me; the fact that it holds no significance for you does not devalue it for me. If someone likes crab apple jelly, then crab apples hold some value for him, although they might be worthless to another person. On this subjective understanding of value it seems likely that music which brings about experiences of the sublime in listeners is valuable to those listeners. Exactly *how* valuable such music is for them will depend in turn on how much value listeners place on their experiences of the sublime. Indeed, there are listeners who positively dislike the feeling of being overwhelmed by music; those who are averse to Wagner's music sometimes cite its "overpowering" character as a factor in their aversion. It is both intuitively obvious and supported by empirical research that people use music for many purposes. They listen in order to cheer themselves up, to relieve the boredom of car trips, to provide a rhythm for household chores or physical exercise. They also listen to music expressly for the sake of listening to it, treating it as an object of aesthetic contemplation. Which of these purposes is more important to a listener can only be judged by him or her.

According to another understanding, "value" is objective: $100 has more value than $1 regardless of the subjective feelings and impressions of any person. I take it as given that some musical works are better than others, both aesthetically better (offering listeners a richer experience) and artistically better (more significant in the history of music, as compared to other works). Part of me wants to endorse the philosopher Nelson Goodman's lofty claim that "works of art are not race-horses, and picking a winner is not the primary goal." Yet judgements about the value of different works of art cannot be as readily dismissed; life is short. If one wants to experience the very best music and art that is available, then critical guidance can help us find those great works more easily than we might on our own. I know that my own engagement with artworks - whether music, literature or visual art - has been immeasurably enriched by the suggestions and counsel of those whose critical acumen is greater than my own.

Assuming that we can at least sometimes make objective assessments of an artwork's value, is music that arouses experiences of the sublime more valuable than music that does not? Is the music that deeply moves listeners simply better music than music that does not, peculiarities of individual listeners aside? Scanning the list of works which have been cited as invoking strong emotional responses - masterworks by Beethoven, Bach, Tchaikovsky and Sibelius - one might be tempted to answer yes. But there are at least two difficulties here. First, there are great works which do not, or do not consistently, arouse experiences of the sublime. Where on the list are Mozart's violin and piano sonatas and string quartets, Handel's *concerti grossi* or Schubert's early symphonies? These are all great works and repay attentive listening, whether or not a listener experiences chills or breaks into tears. Second, the list of works which *do* seem regularly to arouse experiences of the sublime contains many that have not won wide critical approval. It would be arbitrary to take seriously the experiences of those affected by great music and ignore those affected by less than great music. "Extraordinary how potent cheap music is," muses a character in Noël Coward's *Private Lives*. I suspect that the remark is all too apt here.

Are experiences of the sublime in music valuable in the sense that they should be encouraged? Should we make having such experiences one of our aims in listening to music, presuming that this is even possible? One educator has gone so far as to say that the achievement of such experiences is the "ultimate goal" of music education - "encompassing yet transcending all the other goals toward which a good music program aims." Yet there is a tradition, dating at least to Hanslick in the late nineteenth century, which actively *discourages* the cultivation of such responses. Hanslick writes, "the instant music is put to use merely as a means to produce a certain mood in us or as an accessory or an ornament, it ceases to be effective as pure art." The philosopher R. A. Sharpe's more recent declaration is in the same tradition: "The work, not the experience, is the proper focus of attention. Something is wrong if you go to a concert or to the theatre in search of a particular experience." Now, I do not think that the educator quoted above, or indeed anyone, would argue that we should encourage sublime experiences of music as ends in themselves. Such experiences, however rewarding, are not separable from the primary goal of engaging with and understanding music, and everyone recognizes this. But for the sake of the discussion, let us imagine a more extreme version of this position. Imagine a person who listens to certain musical works for the express purpose of having the type of experience we have been considering. Is this person making some kind of mistake? Does she have an objectively less valuable experience than her friend who treats music as an object of aesthetic contemplation?

Sharpe has two main complaints against our imaginary listener who treats music as a means to the end of a sublime (or any other) experience. First, her motivation is suspect. She is like the person who gives to charity because it makes her feel good and she prizes that feeling, rather than giving because there is a need. Sharpe's point is subtle; it is not that we should not feel stirred by music or pleased to give to charity. The point is that we do not listen to music *because* we want to feel stirred or give to charity *because* we want to feel good about ourselves. Those feelings are secondary; if our motivation is "pure" then the good feelings we derive are a bonus. Sharpe's argument, for me, is an example of what can go wrong when arguments from ethics are carried over into aesthetics, especially when the ethical issue is not a matter of firm agreement. (I trust that I am not the only one who finds it unseemly to impugn the motives of those who do good works.) Sharpe's worry about moral motivation is in the tradition of ethical thought inspired by Kant. According to Kant's moral philosophy, the problem with doing a good deed such as giving to charity only because it makes one feel good is that one is liable to behave arbitrarily. If self-satisfaction rather than the alleviation of need is my major motivation, then if I am already pleased with myself, I may feel no further desire to give. If this happens then certainly I will fail in my duty to others. But if I listen to music in order to feel a certain way, and this guides my choice of when and what to listen to, then who is harmed? Whom have I failed? Sharpe, I think, would answer that I have failed myself.

His second complaint against the listener who seeks certain kinds of experiences from music is that such experiences are intrinsically less valuable than the experience afforded by treating music as an object of contemplation. "[W]e judge a set of values as inferior just to the extent that they either prevent somebody from seeing what is great in art or to the extent that they lead him to the wrong set of considerations in judging merit." Sharpe's example is a comment he heard when leaving a Bach concert, to the effect that the music was "restful." By concentrating on restfulness, the listener had missed what can be "interesting and stimulating" in the music. Assuming for the sake of the example that Sharpe's fellow concert-goer was indeed "concentrating" on the music's restfulness rather than merely registering it, has he had a less valuable encounter with the music than the listener who treats it as an object of contemplation? It is tempting to say that he has. Many musical works are conducive to relaxation and relaxation is an estimable pursuit. But the works of Bach are not "many musical works" - they are among the greatest ever composed. Are we right to use them as tranquillizers?

Surely this is to overstate the issue. There is any number of reasons why someone might be taken by a musical work's calming effect rather than by other qualities it possesses. This might say something about a listener's level of musical sophistication and interest, or it might just say something about his current mental state. Thinking back to the spectacularly beautiful iris I mentioned in the previous chapter, if I was rushing to be somewhere on time or mentally agitated or preoccupied by some decision I had to make, I would not stop to look at it. I do not think this means that I am insensitive to beauty; but a neighbour who happened to see me rushing by and ignoring the flower might well conclude that I was. Even if it is true that our "calmed" listener lacks musical sophistication and cannot *hear* the qualities in the music beyond its restfulness, it does not follow that this is his permanent state. A wonderful thing about the modern world is the great variety of recorded music that we can listen to whenever we wish. Maybe the next time he hears the work, or maybe after another hundred hearings, he will have the kind of "pure" disinterested experience that Sharpe endorses and attend to the work's aesthetic qualities. An interest in great musical works has to begin somewhere, and starting with some works because they are "restful" is better than not starting at all. Greater sophistication and discernment can come only through listening.

I was reminded of Sharpe's position and his less than adequate listener when I read some of the comments of commuters who did stop and listen to Bell in the Washington subway. One was John David Mortensen, a project manager in the Department of Energy who was on his way to work. Mortensen was not a fan of classical music and had never before given money to a street musician, or indeed even stopped to listen to a street musician. But he sensed something special about Bell's performance of Bach's "Chaconne" and stopped to listen for three minutes - as long as he possibly could without arriving late for work. When approached later by the newspaper and asked why he stopped, he replied, "Whatever it was, it made me feel at peace." Mortensen did not have the kind of disinterested experience of a musical work that some would argue is optimal; he certainly did not have an experience of the sublime. But the experience was clearly valuable to him, and finding value in something for one's own sake may be a first step to finding it valuable in itself.

ART WITHOUT A FRAME

Let's say I took one of our more abstract masterpieces, say an Ellsworth Kelly, and removed it from its frame, marched it down the 52 steps that people walk up to get to the National Gallery, past the giant columns, and brought it into a restaurant. It's a $5 million painting. And it's one of those restaurants where there are pieces of original art for sale, by some industrious kids from the Corcoran School, and I hang that Kelly on the wall with a price tag of $150. No one is going to notice it. An art curator might look up and say: 'Hey, that looks a little like an Ellsworth Kelly. Please pass the salt.'

Mark Leithauser, Senior curator at the
US National Gallery, quoted in *The Washington Post*

The performances of Bell in the Washington Metro and Little on the London railway bridge are examples of art without a frame - in this

case without an appropriate social context, including the optimal listening conditions we have come to expect for performances of classical
music. Throughout this book I have stressed music's social character. The
Washington and London experiments illustrate what can happen when
music is perceived outside an appropriate social context. People are not
sure how to behave and few are able even to *have* an experience of music.

The usual context for performances of great works by great performers is a concert hall or similar venue, with the pieces to be performed and the identities of the performers clearly indicated. Patrons
choose whether to attend, and usually pay for the privilege. Indeed,
they may plan to attend and pay for tickets months in advance, pre-
arranging babysitting and even vacation plans in order to do so. The
audience knows more or less how long the performance will last, and
they know how they are expected to behave: sit quietly and applaud
at the designated times. The audience have segregated these couple
of hours from the rest of their lives to listen to music and they do
not have to meet any other obligations for the duration of the concert.
Everything about the performance - the silence before the music starts
and during the performance, the comfortable seats, the rapt atmosphere - lends itself to the aesthetic experience. Contrast this with a
performance by a street musician. It happens in an awkward and possibly crowded and noisy place - near public transportation, shops or
other distractions. Depending on the jurisdiction, the performer may
not even have the legal right to perform in public. She is probably
competing with others for our attention and resources. There is often
no place to sit, and standing around can make you feel conspicuous.
We do not know who the performer is or if she is any good. This feeds
into the anxiety that many people have about their own perceived lack
of taste or knowledge. They do not want to be seen by others to be
over-enthusiastic about a mediocre performer or under-appreciative of
a good one. It is safer not to listen and thus not to betray any opinion
at all. We are not informed beforehand which musical works are to be
played. We did not choose to be present at the performance; in fact,
the musician is invading our space and implicitly demanding our time
and attention, if not also our money. And even if we do stop to listen
and enjoy the experience, what would be an appropriate way to show

appreciation? Clap? Say "thank you"? Make a contribution? But how much, and what if it turns out that the only cash you have is an inappropriately large denomination bank note? If you give too little you look stingy; if you give too much you look like an easy mark. All of this makes for a very awkward situation and it is much easier not to stop in the first place. Better to get on with your business.

In both the Washington and London experiments, the journalists involved were impressed by how many children and teenagers were intrigued by the musicians and wanted to stop. Some had to be forcibly carried away by their hurrying parents! The article in the *Independent* describes how "three young lads, no more than 13 years old, wearing baggy jeans and baseball caps, slow in their tracks, gaze at Little, then fumble in their pockets, flushed with self-consciousness. They're determined to give her anything they can, out of their pocket money." Some of the journalists were heartened by the young people's interest and were inspired to draw conclusions about the power of great music. While this may be true, I think something else is going on as well. Children and teenagers are less likely than adults to let their natural curiosity and interest be dampened by the threat of social disapproval or awkwardness. They do not have the preconceived idea that street musicians are not worth their time or that stopping to listen is somehow inappropriate. How else to explain the fact that, in the London experiment, those of the demographic *most* likely to attend classical concerts - well-dressed older men and women - were *least* likely to stop by the railway bridge and listen to Little?

WHY DID ODYSSEUS WEEP?

> Big questions, big questions
> They're bothering you and they're bothering me
> And they even bother people at the BBC
> Big questions, big questions
> > The Jazz Butcher (Patrick Fish), "Conspiracy"

The modern university is a place of academic specialization and segregation. With the exception of social occasions, members of one discipline may have little opportunity to discuss their work with their colleagues in other disciplines. To some extent the management of any large organization requires such compartmentalization. Specialized departments are required to function as "holding tanks" from which teaching can be assigned and where pay cheques can be directed. But specialization and segregation, while making life easier for administrators, have real costs. Disciplinary boundaries can separate people who should really be talking to one another, and indeed who might not even realize that they should be talking to one another. Through much of its history, philosophy has cherished the idea of a synoptic view - a comprehensive vision of how different facets of reality fit together as a whole and affect one another. Aristotle wrote about rhetoric, ethics and politics, about the natural history of animals and the origin of weather patterns. The explosion of learning in the past couple of centuries means that no one in our own time can hope to master all available scientific knowledge in the way that Aristotle was virtually master of all available knowledge in his time. Yet this does not mean that the ideal of a synoptic view has lost its power; only that it is harder to achieve and requires cooperation.

The understanding of music and the effects it can have on us cries out for a collaborative effort and a synoptic view. Different academic specialties, when they take music as their focus, provide a piece of a larger puzzle. Neuroscience can tell us about music's effect on the brain. Psychologists treat music as a cognitive object and can also monitor its effects on the body. Our understanding of the biology of music is enhanced when we consider the work of primate experts and ornithologists. Anthropologists provide a broader picture of the place of music in human culture. The character of particularly absorbing musical works is investigated by musicologists. Music theorists and intellectual historians can shed light on the different attitudes to music held by our ancestors, and show us how those attitudes may or may not inform our own listening habits. Finally, philosophers ask the "big questions" and draw on their own resources, as well as on the work of all of the others, in the hope of providing some answers.

Why should music have an effect on us, let alone be capable of provoking a strong response? Why should music carry any significance for human beings? The answer has to do with music, of course, and the characteristic qualities it has as both a physical stimulus and a cognitive object. But the answers to these questions also have to do with us, and with the kinds of creatures that we human beings are. This book began with the image of Odysseus weeping in response to the song of the great bard Demodocus. A mighty warrior was moved to tears by a song. Why did Odysseus weep? He wept because the music *mattered* to him. The bard's song touched his body and his mind. It connected him with his past and reminded him of significant events in his personal history. And the reasons why the music could do this, and why it could be the sort of thing that would matter to him at all, are intrinsically bound up with the kind of thing that music is and always has been. Music and musical experience are social through and through. From infancy and throughout the rest of our lives, in ritual and other social settings, it is part of the social processes that enmesh us. It thus has very deep roots in our upbringing and socialization, both cognitive and emotional. This has to be why everything, from "cheap music," through patriotic and folk songs, to the most demanding art music, has the power to inspire strong emotional responses. The range of responses to music includes everything from weeping at hearing the folk songs of a distant past, through chills, through deep yet quiet awe. Usually, we reserve the term "sublime" for extraordinary reactions to certain masterworks and virtuoso performances. We do not know what the tune that Demodocus sang sounded like, but we do know that he was the bard whom the Muses loved above all others. This was a Greek way of saying that Demodocus was a supreme artist. Odysseus could not simply close his ears and refuse to hear the music. The aesthetic power of the bard's song was such that it imposed itself on his consciousness. He simply could not shut it out; though he was a fierce and cunning warrior, the song penetrated his defences.

The music Demodocus played and sang must have been special and perhaps we can hardly imagine what it sounded like, given the thousands of years that have passed and the cultural gulfs that separate us from that time. But Homer lets us know that music mattered to Odysseus and we have no reason to think that he was in this respect so very different from us. Music is part of our humanity: It is connected to our emotional repertoire, to our cognitive skills, and in it we can give expression to that urge to transcend that gives birth to the most sublime art.

BIBLIOGRAPHIC NOTES

PREFACE

Stephen Davies, "Philosophical Perspectives on Music's Expressiveness," in *Music and Emotion: Theory and Research*, eds. Patrik N. Juslin and John A. Sloboda (Oxford: Oxford University Press, 2001), pp. 23-44.

Vladimir J. Konečni, Review of *Music and Emotion: Theory and Research*, eds. Patrik N. Juslin and John A. Sloboda, *Music Perception* 20 (Spring 2003) 332-41.

Vladimir J. Konečni, Amber Brown and Rebekah A. Wanic, "Comparative Effects of Music and Recalled Life-events on Emotional State," *Psychology of Music* (2007) 1-20.

Vladimir J. Konečni, "Does Music Induce Emotion? A Theoretical and Methodological Analysis," *Psychology of Aesthetics, Creativity, and the Arts* (in press).

Vladimir J. Konečni, "The Influence of Affect on Music Choice," forthcoming in *Music and Emotion: Theory and Research*, 2nd edn., eds. Patrik N. Juslin and John A. Sloboda (Oxford: Oxford University Press).

Joseph LeDoux, *The Emotional Brain: The Mysterious Underpinnings of Emotional Life* (New York: Simon & Schuster, 1998).

Jerrold Levinson, "Musical Chills and Other Musical Delights," in *The Musical Practitioner* ed. J. Davidson (Aldershot: Ashgate, 2004), pp. 335-51.

Jaak Panksepp, "The Emotional Sources of 'Chills' Induced by Music," *Music Perception* 13:2 (Winter 1995) 171-207.

John A. Sloboda and Patrik N. Juslin, "Psychological Perspectives on Music and Emotion," in *Music and Emotion: Theory and Research*, eds. Patrik N. Juslin and John A. Sloboda (Oxford: Oxford University Press, 2001), pp. 71-104.

1 THE TEARS OF ODYSSEUS

Aristotle, *The Politics*, trans. T.A. Sinclair (London: Penguin Books, 1981).

Augustine, *Confessions*, trans. R.S. Pine-Coffin (Baltimore, MD: Penguin Books, 1961).

Boethius, *On Music* in *Contemplating Music: Source Readings in the Aesthetics of Music*, Volume I, eds. Ruth Katz and Carl Dahlhaus (Stuyvesant, NY: Pendragon Press, 1987).

Gretchen L. Finney, "Ecstasy and Music in Seventeenth-Century England," *Journal of the History of Ideas* 8:2 (April 1947) 153-86.

Gretchen L. Finney " 'Organical Musick' and Ecstasy," *Journal of the History of Ideas* 8:3 (June 1947) 273-92.

Bill Friskies-Warren, *I'll Take You There: Pop Music and the Urge for Transcendence* (New York: Continuum, 2005).

Nelson Goodman, *Languages of Art* (Indianapolis: Hackett, 1976).

Theodore Gracyk, *I Wanna Be Me: Rock Music and the Politics of Identity* (Philadelphia: Temple University Press, 2001).

Kathleen Marie Higgins, *The Music of Our Lives* (Philadelphia: Temple University Press, 1991).

Homer, *The Odyssey*, trans. E. V. Rieu (Baltimore, MD: Penguin Books, 1956).

Justine Kingsbury, "Matravers on Musical Expressiveness," *British Journal of Aesthetics* 42:1 (January 2002) 13-19.

Peter Kivy, "Feeling the Musical Emotions," *British Journal of Aesthetics* 39:1 (January 1999) 1-13.

Peter Kivy, *Sound Sentiment* (Philadelphia: Temple University Press, 1989).

Vladimir J. Konečni, "The Aesthetic Trinity: Awe, Being Moved, Thrills," *Bulletin of Psychology and the Arts* 5:2 (2005) 27-44.

Jerrold Levinson, "The Concept of Music," in *Music, Art, and Metaphysics: Essays in Philosophical Aesthetics* (Ithaca, NY: Cornell University Press, 1990), pp. 267-78.

Derek Matravers, *Art and Emotion* (Oxford: Clarendon Press, 1998).

Derek Matravers, "Musical Expressiveness," *Philosophy Compass* 2/3 (2007) 373-9.

Bruno Nettl, *Music in Primitive Culture* (Cambridge, MA: Harvard University Press, 1972).

Bruno Nettl, *The Study of Ethnomusicology: Twenty-nine Issues and Concepts* (Urbana, IL: University of Illinois Press, 1983).

Bruno Nettl, "An Ethnomusicologist Contemplates Universals in Musical Sound and Musical Culture," in *The Origins of Music*, eds. Nils L. Wallin, Björn Merker and Steven Brown (Cambridge, MA: MIT Press, 2001), pp. 463-72.

Plato, *Complete Works*, ed. John M. Cooper (Indianapolis: Hackett, 1997).

Gilbert Rouget, *Music and Trance: A Theory of the Relations between Music and Possession*, trans. Brunhilde Biebuyck (Chicago: University of Chicago Press, 1985).

Amnon Shiloah, *Music in the World of Islam: A Socio-cultural Study* (Detroit: Wayne State University Press, 1995).

Benedict Spinoza, *The Ethics and Selected Letters*, trans. Samuel Shirley (Indianapolis: Hackett, 1987).

Jan Swafford, *The Vintage Guide to Classical Music* (New York: Vintage Books, 1992).

Julian Young, "Death and Transfiguration: Kant, Schopenhauer and Heidegger on the Sublime," *Inquiry* 48:2 (April 2005) 131-44.

Nick Zangwill, "Against Emotion: Hanslick was Right about Music," *British Journal of Aesthetics* 44:1 (January 2004) 29-43.

2 HISTORY

M. H. Abrams, "Art-as-Such: The Sociology of Modern Aesthetics," in *Doing Things with Texts: Essays in Criticism and Critical Theory*, ed. Michael Fisher (New York: W.W. Norton, 1989), pp. 135-58.

Mark Evan Bonds, *Music as Thought: Listening to the Symphony in the Age of Beethoven* (Princeton, NJ: Princeton University Press, 2006).

Leon Botstein, "Towards a History of Listening," *The Musical Quarterly* 82:3/4 (Autumn-Winter 1998) 427-31.

J. T. Boulton, "Introduction," *A Philosophical Enquiry into the Origin of our Ideas of the Sublime and Beautiful* by Edmund Burke (London: Routledge & Kegan Paul, 1958).

Edmund Burke, *A Philosophical Enquiry into the Origin of our Ideas of the Sublime and Beautiful* (London: Routledge & Kegan Paul, 1958).

Carl Dahlhaus, *The Idea of Absolute Music*, trans. Roger Lustig (Chicago: University of Chicago Press, 1989).

Lydia Goehr, "Schopenhauer and the Musicians," in *Schopenhauer, Philosophy, and the Arts*, ed. Dale Jacquette (Cambridge: Cambridge University Press, 1996), pp. 200-28.

Eduard Hanslick, *On the Musically Beautiful*, trans. Geoffrey Payzant (Indianpolis: Hackett, 1986).

James J. Hill, "The Aesthetic Principles of the *Peri Hupsous*," *Journal of the History of Ideas* 27:2 (April-June 1966) 265-74.

Allan Janik and Stephen Toulmin, *Wittgenstein's Vienna* (New York: Simon & Schuster, 1973).

James H. Johnson, *Listening in Paris, a Cultural History* (Berkeley, CA: University of California Press, 1995).

E. T. A. Hoffmann, "Beethoven's Instrumental Music," in R. Murray Schafer, *E.T.A. Hoffmann and Music* (Toronto: University of Toronto Press, 1975).

Immanuel Kant, *Critique of Judgement* trans. J. H. Bernard (New York: Hafner Press, 1951).

Peter Kivy, *The Possessor and the Possessed: Handel, Mozart, Beethoven, and the Idea of Musical Genius* (New Haven, CT: Yale University Press, 2001).

Jerrold Levinson, "Schopenhauer," *Encyclopedia of Aesthetics*, ed. Michael Kelly, Vol. 4 (Oxford: Oxford University Press, 1998), pp. 245-50.

Longinus, *On the Sublime*, trans. H. L. Havell, *Essays in Classical Criticism* (London: J.M. Dent and Sons, 1953).

Richard Macksey, "Longinus Reconsidered," *Modern Language Notes* 108:5 (December 1993) 913-34.

Bryan Magee, *The Philosophy of Schopenhauer* (Oxford: Clarendon Press, 1997).

Rudolf Makkreel, "Imagination and Temporality in Kant's Theory of the Sublime," *Journal of Aesthetics and Art Criticism* 42 (1984) 303-15.

R. Meager, "The Sublime and the Obscene," *British Journal of Aesthetics* 4 (July 1964) 214-27.

Samuel H. Monk, *The Sublime: A Study of Critical Theories in XVIII-Century England* (Ann Arbor, MI: University of Michigan Press, 1960).

John Neubauer, *The Emancipation of Music from Language: Departure from Mimesis in Eighteennth-Century Aesthetics* (New Haven, CT: Yale University Press, 1986).

Marjorie Hope Nicolson, *Mountain Gloom and Mountain Glory: The Development of the Aesthetics of the Infinite* (New York: W.W. Norton, 1959).

Herman Parret, "Kant on Music and the Hierarchy of the Arts," *Journal of Aesthetics and Art Criticism* 56:3 (Summer 1998) 251-64.

Vanessa L. Ryan, "The Physiological Sublime: Burke's Critique of Reason," *Journal of the History of Ideas* 62:2 (April 2001) 265-79.

Greg Sandow, "When Mozart Went to Paris." http://www.gregsandow.com/mozpar.htm. Accessed August 7, 2007.

A. Schopenhauer, *The World as Will and Representation* 2 Volumes trans. E. F. J. Payne (New York: Dover Publications, 1966).

H. Schueller, "The Pleasures of Music: Speculation in British Music Criticism 1750-1800," *Journal of Aesthetics and Art Criticism* 8:3 (March 1950) 155-71.

Roger Scruton, *Kant* (Oxford: Oxford University Press, 1982).

Jerome Stolnitz, "On the Origins of 'Aesthetic Disinterestedness'," *Journal of Aesthetics and Art Criticism* 20:42 (Winter 1961) 131-43.

Bart Vandenabeele, "Schopenhauer on the Beautiful and the Sublime: A Qualitative or Gradual Distinction?" *Schopenhauer Jahrbuch* 82 (2001) 99-112.

Bart Vandenabeele, "Schopenhauer, Nietzsche, and the Aesthetically Sublime," *Journal of Aesthetic Education* 37:1 (Spring 2003) 90-106.

Richard Wagner, *Wagner on Music and Drama*, eds. Albert Goldman and Evert Sprinchorn, trans. H. Ashton Ellis (London: Gollancz, 1970).

George B. Walsh, "Sublime Method: Longinus on Language and Imitation," *Classical Antiquity* 7:2 (October 1988) 252-69.

William Weber, "Did People Listen in the 18th Century?" *Early Music* 25:4 (November 1997) 678-91.

3 TEARS, CHILLS AND BROKEN BONES

Madame Verderin's response to Vinteuil's (fictional) piano sonata is described in:
Marcel Proust, *Remembrance of Things Past*, Volume 1, trans. C. K. Scott Moncrieff and Terence Kilmartin (London: Chatto & Windus, 1981), pp. 223-5.

I have borrowed the term "strong experiences of music" from Gabrielsson's "Strong Experiences of Music" (SEM) Project. For this and much else I am greatly in their debt. Information about the SEM Project and its results can be found in:

A. Gabrielsson, "Emotions and Strong Experiences with Music," in *Music and Emotion: Theory and Research*, eds. Patrik N. Juslin and John A. Sloboda (Oxford: Oxford University Press, 2001), pp. 431-49.

A. Gabrielsson, "Strong Experiences Elicited by Music - What Music?" in *New Directions in Aesthetics, Creativity, and the Arts*, eds. Paul Locher, Colin Martindale and Leonid Dorfman (Amityville, NY: Baywood, 2006), pp. 253-69.

A. Gabrielsson and S. Lindström, "On Strong Experiences of Music," *Musik Psychologie* 10 (1993) 118-39.

A. Gabrielsson and S. Lindström, "Can Strong Experiences of Music have Therapeutic Implications?" in *Music and the Mind Machine: The Psychophysiology and Psychopathology of the Sense of Music*, ed. R. Steinberg, (Berlin: Springer-Verlag, 1995), pp. 195-202.

A. Gabrielsson and S. Lindström Wik, "Strong Experiences of and with Music," in *Musicology and Sister Disciplines: Past, Present, Future*. eds. David Greer, Ian Rumbold and Jonathan King (Oxford: Oxford University Press, 2000), pp. 100-8.

A. Gabrielsson and S. Lindström Wik, "Strong Experiences Related to Music: A Descriptive System," *Musicae Scientiae* 7:2 (Fall 2003) 157-217.

The remaining descriptions of emotionally strong responses to music are taken from the following sources. They are listed in the order that they appear in the text.

John Seabrook, "The Money Note: Can the Record Business Survive?" *The New Yorker* (July 7, 2003), p. 45.

James Elkins, *Pictures and Tears: A History of People who have Cried in Front of Paintings* (New York: Routledge, 2001), p. 248.

Ted Bond, personal communication.

Bill Donahue, "Under the Sheltering Sky," *The Washington Post Magazine* (September 21, 2003), 34.

Robert Panzarella, "The Phenomenology of Aesthetic Peak Experiences," *Humanistic Psychology* 20:1 (1980) 76.

Bryan Magee, *Confessions of a Philosopher* (London: Weidenfeld & Nicolson, 1997), pp. 281-2.

John Sloboda, "Music as a Language," in *Music and Child Development*, eds. F. Wilson and F. Roehmann (St. Louis, MO: MMB, 1989), p. 37.

Jean-Jacques Rousseau *Dictionnaire de musique* (New York: Johnson Reprint Corporation, 1969), p. 314. The translation quoted is from Gilbert Rouget, *Music and Trance: A Theory of the Relations between Music and Possession*, trans. Brunhilde Biebuyck (Chicago: University of Chicago Press, 1985), p. 168.

Simon Jargy, *La Musique arabe* (Paris: Presses universitaires de France, 1971), pp. 25-6. The translation quoted is from Gilbert Rouget, *Music and Trance: A Theory of the Relations between Music and Possession*, trans. Brunhilde Biebuyck (Chicago: University of Chicago Press, 1985), p. 281.

4 THE MUSIC ITSELF

I consulted the following works for the section on music and trance states:

Aristotle, *The Politics*, trans. T.A. Sinclair and Trevor J. Saunders (Harmondsworth: Penguin Books, 1981).

Jörg Fachner, "Music and Altered States of Consciousness: An Overview," in *Music and Altered States: Consciousness, Transcendence, Therapy and Addictions*, eds. David Aldridge and Jörg Fachner (London: Jessica Kingsley, 2006), pp. 15-37.

David Fanshawe. Liner notes to *Witchcraft & Ritual Music*, Nonesuch Explorer Series 79708-2. 1975

Plato, *Symposium*, trans. Alexander Nehemas and Paul Woodruff (Indianapolis: Hackett, 1989).

Gilbert Rouget, *Music and Trance: A Theory of the Relations between Music and Possession*, trans. Brunhilde Biebuyck (Chicago: University of Chicago Press, 1985).

I discuss the following psychological studies in this chapter:

Martin Guhn, Alfons Hamm and Marcel Zentner, "Physiological and Musico-acoustic Correlates of the Chill Response," *Music Perception* 24:5 (2007): 473-83.

Vladimir J. Konečni, Rebekah A. Wanic and Amber Brown, "Emotional and Aesthetic Antecedents and Consequences of Music-Induced Thrills," *American Journal of Psychology* 120:4 (2007) 619-43.

Michael J. Lowis, "Music and Peak Experiences: An Empirical Study," *The Mankind Quarterly* 39:2 (Winter 1998) 203-24.

Jaak Panksepp, "The Emotional Sources of 'Chills' Induced by Music," *Music Perception* 13:2 (Winter 1995) 171-207.

Nikki S. Rickard, "Intense Emotional Responses to Music: A Test of the Physiological Arousal Hypothesis," *Psychology of Music* 32:4 (2004) 371-88.

Klaus R. Scherer, Marcel Zentner and Annekathrin Schacht, "Emotional States Generated by Music: An Exploratory Study of Music Experts," *Musicae Scientiae* (Special Issue 2001-2) 149-71.

John Sloboda, "Music Structure and Emotional Response: Some Empirical Findings," *Psychology of Music* 19 (1991) 110-20.

Other works consulted:

Donald Clarke, ed. *The Penguin Encyclopedia of Popular Music* (Harmondsworth: Penguin Books, 1989). The quotation on Pink Floyd is on pp. 918-19.

Patrik N. Juslin and John A. Sloboda, "Music and Emotion: Introduction," in *Music and Emotion: Theory and Research*, eds. Patrik N. Juslin and John A. Sloboda (Oxford: Oxford University Press, 2001), pp. 3-20.

Jerrold Levinson, "Musical Chills and Other Musical Delights," in *The Musical Practitioner*, ed. J. Davidson (Aldershot: Ashgate, 2004), pp. 335-51.

Michel Poizat, *The Angel's Cry: Beyond the Pleasure Principle in Opera*, trans. Arthur Denner (Ithaca, NY: Cornell University Press, 1992).

Colin Radford, "How Can Music be Moral?" *Midwest Studies in Philosophy* 16 (1991) 421-38.

R. A. Sharpe, *Philosophy of Music: An Introduction* (Stocksfield: Acumen Publishing, 2004).

Anne Vincent-Buffault, *The History of Tears: Sensibility and Sentimentality in France*, trans. Teresa Bridgeman (New York: St. Martin's Press, 1991). The quotation about the nineteenth-century *Grand Larousse* is on p. 197.

The recordings I mentioned are:

"Witchcraft and Ritual Music" (Nonesuch Explorer Series 79708-2)

Yuri Temirkanov (82876-62320-2 RCA Red Seal Classic Library)

5 EXPLAINING STRONG RESPONSES TO MUSIC

Frank Zappa tells the story about his music teacher in:

Frank Zappa with Peter Occhiogrosso, *The Real Frank Zappa Book* (New York: Poseidon Press, 1989), p. 35.

I first read about Zappa's story in:

Theodore Gracyk, *I Wanna Be Me: Rock Music and the Politics of Identity*, (Philadelphia: Temple University Press, 2001).

The terminology: "pharmaceutical model of musical understanding" comes from:

John Sloboda, "Everyday Uses of Music Listening: A Preliminary Survey," in *Music, Mind, and Science*, ed. Suk Won Yi (Seoul: Seoul National University Press, 1999), pp. 354-5.

Also relevant is the discussion is:

René Descartes, *Compendium of Music*, trans. Walter Robert (Middleton, WI: American Institute of Musicology, 1991).

Réné Descartes, *Oeuvres de Descartes*, Volume I, eds. C. Adam and P. Tannery (Paris: Vrin, 1965), p. 142.

Peter Kivy, *Music Alone: Philosophical Reflections of the Purely Musical Experience* (Ithaca, NY: Cornell University Press, 1994), pp. 30-41.

I consulted the following works for the section on drumming and trance states:

E. D. Adrian and B. H. C. Matthews, "The Berger Rhythm: Potential Changes for the Occipital Lobes in Man," *Brain* 4:57 (December 1934), 355-85.

Additional information about Berger can be found at: http://chem.ch.huji.ac.il/~eugeniik/history/berger.html.

Fachner, Jörg, "Music and Altered States of Consciousness," in *Music and Altered States: Consciousness, Transcendence, Therapy and Addictions*, eds. David Aldridge and Jörg Fachner (London: Jessica Kingsley, 2006), pp. 15-37.

Andrew Neher, "Auditory Driving Observed with Scalp Electrodes in Normal Subjects," *Electroencephalography and Clinical Neurophysiology* 13 (1961) 449-51.

Andrew Neher, "A Physiological Explanation of Unusual Behavior in Ceremonies Involving Drums," *Human Biology* 4: 151-60.

A detailed critique of Neher's hypothesis can be found in Gilbert Rouget, *Music and Trance: A Theory of the Relations Between Music and Possession*, trans. Brunhilde Biebuyck (Chicago: University of Chicago Press, 1985), pp. 172-6.

Michael Winkelman, "Trance States: A Theoretical Model and Cross-Cultural Analysis," *Ethos* 14:2 (Summer 1986) 174-203.

Lisa N. Woodside, V. K. Kumar and Ronald J. Pekala, "Monotonous Percussion Drumming and Trance Postures: A Controlled Evaluation of Phenomenological Effects," *Anthropology of Consciousness* 8: 2-3 (1997) 69-87.

Other works consulted in this chapter:

Dean Falk, "Hominid Brain Evolution and the Origins of Music," in *The Origins of Music*, eds. Nils L. Wallin, Björn Merkur and Steven Brown (Cambridge, MA: MIT Press, 2001), pp. 197-216.

Grewe, Oliver et al., "Listening to Music as a Re-creative Process: Physiological, Psychological, and Psychacoustical Correlates of Chills and Strong Emotions," *Music Perception* 24:3 (2007) 297-314.

Daniel J Levitin, *This is Your Brain on Music: The Science of a Human Obsession* (New York: Dutton, 2006).

Tom Lutz, *Crying: the Natural and Cultural History of Tears* (New York: W.W. Norton, 1999).

Leonard B. Meyer, *Emotion and Meaning in Music* (Chicago: University of Chicago Press, 1956).

Claudio Robazza, Cristina Macaluso and Valentina D'Urso, "Emotional Reactions to Music by Gender, Age, and Expertise," *Perceptual and Motor Skills* 79 (1994) 939-44.

John Sloboda, "Empirical Studies of Emotional Response to Music," in *Cognitive Bases of Musical Communication*, eds. Mari Riess Jones and Susan Holleran (Washington, DC: American Psychological Association, 1992), pp. 33-46.

Anne Vincent-Buffault, *The History of Tears: Sensibility and Sentimentality in France*, trans. Teresa Bridgeman (New York: St. Martin's Press, 1991).

6 EXPLAINING STRONG RESPONSES TO MUSIC

I explored some of these issues in a preliminary manner in:

Jeanette Bicknell, "Explaining Strong Emotional Responses to Music: Sociality and Intimacy," *Journal of Consciousness Studies* 14:12 (2007) 5-23.

Due to the length of this chapter and the number of sources consulted, I have arranged the references by section.

Music and the Social World

Aristotle, *Politics*, 1253a1-5.

Ruth Benedict, *The Chrysanthemum and the Sword: Patterns of Japanese Culture* (New York: New American Library, 1974).

R. Cox, "Are Musical Works Discovered?" *Journal of Aesthetics and Art Criticism* 43 (1985) 367-74.

Terrence W. Deacon, *The Symbolic Species: The Co-evolution of Language and the Brain* (New York: W.W. Norton, 1997).

Ellen Dissanayake, "Becoming *Homo Aestheticus*: Sources of Aesthetic Imagination in Mother-Infant Interactions," *SubStance* 94/95 (2001) 85-103.

Robin Dunbar, "Coevolution of neocortical size, group size and language in humans," *Behavioral and Brain Sciences* 16 (1993) 681-735

François Lesure, *Music and Art in Society*, trans. Denis and Sheila Stevens (University Park: Pennsylvania State University Press, 1968).

Bruno Nettle, "An Ethnomusicologist Contemplates Universals in Musical Sound and Musical Culture," in *The Origins of Music*, eds. Nils L. Wallin, Björn Merkur and Steven Brown (Cambridge, MA: MIT Press, 2001), pp. 463-72.

Michel Poizat, *The Angel's Cry: Beyond the Pleasure Principle in Opera*, trans. Arthur Denner (Ithaca, NY: Cornell University Press, 1992).

Bennett Reimer, "The Experience of Profundity in Music," *Journal of Aesthetic Education* 29:4 (Winter 1995) 1-21.

John Sloboda, "Everyday Uses of Music Listening: A Preliminary Survey," in *Music, Mind, and Science*, ed. Suk Won Yi (Seoul: Seoul National University Press, 1999), pp. 354-69.

Benedict Spinoza, *Ethics*, III, Definition of the emotions, 31.

Ludwig Wittgenstein, *Philosophical Investigations*, trans. G. E. M. Anscombe (Oxford: Basil Blackwell, 1953). The relevant sections are 243-315.

Music and Social Bonding

Simha Arom, "Prolegomena to a Biomusicology," in *The Origins of Music*, eds. Nils L. Wallin, Björn Merkur and Steven Brown (Cambridge, MA: MIT Press, 2001), pp. 27-8.

John Bowlby, *Attachment and Loss*, 3 Volumes (London: Hogarth Press, 1969).

Charles Darwin, *The Descent of Man and Selection in Relation to Sex* , 2nd edn. (London: John Murray, 1882).

Ellen Dissanayake, "Antecedents of the Temporal Arts in Early Mother-Infant Interaction," in *The Origins of Music*, eds. Nils L. Wallin, Björn Merkur and Steven Brown (Cambridge, MA: MIT Press, 2001), pp. 389-410.

W. Tecumseh Fitch, "The Biology and Evolution of Music: A Comparative Perspective," *Cognition* 100 (2006) 173-215.

Thomas Geissmann, "Gibbon Songs and Human Music from an Evolutionary Perspective," in *The Origins of Music*, eds. Nils L. Wallin, Björn Merkur and Steven Brown (Cambridge, MA: MIT Press, 2001), pp. 103-23.

Kathleen Higgins, *The Music of our Lives* (Philadelphia: Temple University Press, 1991).

Adrian C. North, David J. Hargreaves and Susan A. O'Neill, "The Importance of Music to Adolescents," *British Journal of Educational Psychology* 70 (2000) 255-72.

Jaak Panksepp, "Affective Consciousness. Core Emotional Feelings in Animals and Humans," *Consciousness and Cognition* 14 (2005) 30-80.

Isabelle Peretz, "The Nature of Music from a Biological Perspective," *Cognition* 100 (2006) 1-32.

Sandra E. Trehub, "Human Processing Predispositions and Musical Universals," in *The Origins of Music*, eds. Nils L. Wallin, Björn Merkur and Steven Brown (Cambridge, MA: MIT Press, 2001), pp. 427-48.

Sandra Trehub and Takayuki Nakata, "Emotion and Music in Infancy," *Musicae Scientiae* (Special Issue 2001-2) 37-61.

Sandra E. Trehub, Anna M. Unyk et al., "Mothers' and Fathers' Singing to Infants," *Developmental Psychology* 33:3 (1997), 500-7.

Music, Emotion and The Brain: (1) General

BBC News, "Music 'can aid stroke recovery,'" http://news.bbc.co.uk/2/hi/health/7250594. stm. Accessed February 20, 2008.

Anne J. Blood et al., "Emotional Responses to Pleasant and Unpleasant Music Correlate with Activity in Paralimbic Brain Regions," *Nature Neuroscience* 2:4 (April 1999) 382-7.

Anne J. Blood and Robert J. Zatorre, "Intensely Pleasurable Responses to Music Correlate with Activity in Brain Regions Implicated in Reward and Emotion," *PNAS* 98:20 (September 25, 2001) 11818-23.

Nathalie Gosselin, Isabelle Peretz, et al., "Impaired Recognition of Scary Music Following Unilateral Temporal Lobe Excision," *Brain* 128 (2005) 628-40.

Theodore Gracyk, *I Wanna Be Me: Rock Music and the Politics of Identity* (Philadelphia: Temple University Press, 2001). This is the source of the Keith Richards quotation.

Vladimir J. Konečni, Rebekah A. Wanic and Amber Brown, "Emotional and Aesthetic Antecedents and Consequences of Music-induced Thrills," *American Journal of Psychology* 120:4 (2007) 619-43.

C. L. Krumhansl, "An Exploratory Study of Musical Emotions and Psychophysiology," *Canadian Journal of Experimental Psychology* 51 (1997) 336-52.

Joseph LeDoux, *The Emotional Brain: The Mysterious Underpinnings of Emotional Life* (New York: Simon & Schuster, 1998).

LiveScience Staff, "Music During Surgery Reduces Sedation Needs," http://www.livescience.com/health/050525_music_surgery.html. Accessed February 20, 2008.

V. Menon and D. J. Levitin, "The Rewards of Music Listening: Response and Physiological Connectivity of the Mesolimbic System," *NeuroImage* 28 (2005) 175-84.

Jaak Panksepp and Günther Bernatzky, "Emotional Sounds and the Brain: The Neuroaffective Foundations of Musical Appreciation," *Behavioural Processes* 60 (2002) 133-55.

I. Peretz et al. "Music and Emotion: Perceptual Determinant, Immediacy, and Isolation after Brain Damage," *Cognition* 68 (1998) 111-41.

I. Peretz and L. Gagnon, "Dissociation between Recognitional and Emotional Judgements for Melodies," Neurocase 5 (1999) 21-30.

I. Peretz and R. J. Zatorre, "Brain Organization for Music Processing," *Annual Review of Psychology* 56 (2005) 89-114.

Oliver Sacks and Concetta M. Tomaino, "Music and Neurological Disorder," *International Journal of Arts Medicine* 1:1 (Fall 1991) 10-12.

Donald Scott, "Musicogenic Epilepsy (2) The Later Story," in *Music and the Brain: Studies in the Neurology of Music*, eds. MacDonald Critchey and R. A. Henson (London: William Heinemann Medical Books, 1977), pp. 354-64.

A. Storr, *Music and the Mind* (New York: Free Press, 1992).

Music, Emotion and The Brain: (2) The Neurobiology of Attachment

Sue Carter, "Neuroendocrine Perspectives on Social Attachment and Love," *Psychoneuroendocrinology* 23:8 (November 1998) 779-818.

Antonio Damasio, *Descartes' Error: Emotion, Reason, and the Human Brain* (New York: Avon Books, 1994).

Antonio Damasio, *The Feeling of What Happens: Body and Emotion in the Making of Consciousness* (San Diego: Harcourt, 1999).

Scott R. Hutson, "Technoshamanism: Spiritual Healing in the Rave Subculture," *Popular Music and Society* 23 (1999) 53-77.

Thomas R. Insel, "Oxytocin and the Neurobiology of Attachment," *Behavioral and Brain Sciences* 15 (1992) 515-16.

T. R. Insel, "A Neurobiological Basis of Social Attachment," *American Journal of Psychiatry* 154 (1997) 726-35.

Jaak Panksepp, "The Emotional Sources of 'Chills' Induced by Music," *Music Perception* 13:2 (Winter 1995) 171-207.

Marla Vacek, "High on Fidelity," *American Scientist Online.* http://www.americanscientist.org/template/AssetDetail/assetid/14756. Accessed July 12, 2005.

Walter Freeman, *Societies of Brains: A Study in the Neuroscience of Love and Hate* (Hillsdale, NJ: Lawrence Erlbaum, 1995).

Walter Freeman, *How Brains Make up Their Minds* (London: Weidenfeld & Nicolson, 1999).

Walter Freeman, "A Neurobiological Role of Music in Social Bonding," in *The Origins of Music,* eds. Nils L. Wallin, Björn Merkur and Steven Brown (Cambridge, MA: MIT Press, 2001), pp. 411-24.

Music and the Mind: Cognitive Approaches

William Benzon, *Beethoven's Anvil: Music in Mind and Culture* (New York: Basic Books, 2001).

Lev Vygotsky, *Thought and Language* (Cambridge, MA: MIT Press, 1986).

Music and Social Bonding (Again): Intimacy

David Aldridge, "Music, Consciousness and Altered States," in *Music and Altered States: Consciousness, Transcendence, Therapy and Addictions* eds. David Aldridge and Jörg Fachner (London: Jessica Kingsley, 2006), pp. 8-14.

Frances Berenson, "Inter-cultural Understanding and Art," *Nordisk Estetisk Tidskrift* 8 (1992) 5-16.

Ted Cohen, *Jokes: Philosophical Thoughts on Joking Matters* (Chicago: University of Chicago Press, 1999).

Robert S. Gerstein, "Intimacy and Privacy," *Ethics* 89:1 (October 1978) 76-81.

Jerrold Levinson, "Music and Negative Emotion," in *Music, Art, and Metaphysics: Essays in Philosophical Aesthetics* (Ithaca, NY: Cornell University Press, 1990), pp. 306-35.

Jerrold Levinson and Philip Alperson, "What is a Temporal Art?" *Midwest Studies in Philosophy* 16 (1991) 439-50.

Daniel J Levitin, *This is Your Brain on Music: The Science of a Human Obsession* (New York: Dutton, 2006).

R. A. Sharpe, *Philosophy of Music: An Introduction* (Stocksfield: Acumen Publishing, 2004).

7 THE SUBLIME, REVISITED

Jeanette Bicknell, "Music, Listeners, and Moral Awareness," *Philosophy Today* 45 (Fall 2001) 266-74, where I wrote about the connections between music and morality.

E. F. Carritt, *The Theory of Beauty* (London: Methuen, 1962).

Stephen Davies, "Profundity in Instrumental Music," *British Journal of Aesthetics* 42:4 (October 2002) 343-56.

Eduard Hanslick, *On the Musically Beautiful,* trans. Geoffrey Payzant (Indianapolis: Hackett, 1986).

Immanuel Kant, *Critique of Judgement,* trans. J.H. Bernard (New York: Hafner Press, 1951).

Peter Kivy, *Music Alone: Philosophical Reflections of the Purely Musical Experience* (Ithaca, NY: Cornell University Press, 1994).

Peter Kivy, "Another Go at Musical Profundity: Stephen Davies and the Game of Chess," *British Journal of Aesthetics* 43:4 (October 2003), pp. 401-11.

Deborah Knight, "Why We Enjoy Condemning Sentimentality," *Journal of Aesthetics and Art Criticism* 57:4 (1999).

Jerrold Levinson, "Musical Profundity Misplaced," *Journal of Aesthetics and Art Criticism* 50:1 (Winter 1992) 58-60.

Longinus, On the Sublime, trans. H. L. Havell, Essays in Classical Criticsm (London: Dent, 1953).

Leonard Meyer, "Some Remarks on Value and Greatness in Music," in *Music, the Arts and Ideas: Patterns and Predictions in Twentieth-Century Culture* (Chicago: University of Chicago Press, 1967), pp. 22–41.

Mary Mothersill, *Beauty Restored* (Oxford: Clarendon Press, 1984).

Mary Mothersill, "Sublime," in *A Companion to Aesthetics*, ed. David Cooper (Oxford: Blackwell, 1997), pp. 407-12.

Mary Mothersill, "Beauty and the Critic's Judgment: Remapping Aesthetics," in *The Blackwell Guide to Aesthetics* ed. Peter Kivy (Oxford: Blackwell, 2004), pp. 152-66.

Ira Newman, "Learning from Tolstoy: Forgetfulness and Recognition in Literary Edification," *Philosophia* 36:1 (March 2008) 43-54.

Colin Radford, "How Can Music Be Moral?" *Midwest Studies in Philosophy* 16 (1991) 421-38.

Bennett Reimer, "The Experience of Profundity in Music," *Journal of Aesthetic Education* 29:4 (Winter 1995) 1-21.

Aaron Ridley, *The Philosophy of Music: Theme and Variations* (Edinburgh: Edinburgh University Press, 2004).

Roger Scruton, *The Aesthetics of Music* (Oxford: Clarendon Press, 1998).

R. A. Sharpe, "Sounding the Depths," *British Journal of Aesthetics* 40:1 (January 2000) 64-72.

Guy Sircello, *A New Theory of Beauty* (Princeton, NJ: Princeton University Press, 1975).

David A. White, "Towards a Theory of Profundity in Music," *Journal of Aesthetics and Art Criticism* 50 (1992) 23-34.

CONCLUSION - VALUES

Jeanette Bicknell, Review of R. A. Sharpe, *Philosophy of Music: An Introduction*, *British Journal of Aesthetics* 45:4 (October 2005): 447-8.

Jessica Duchen, "Tasmin Little: Playing Great Music in Unexpected Locations," *The Independent* http://www.independent.co.uk/arts-entertainment/music/features/tasmin-little-playing-great-music-in-unexpected-locations-445377.html. Accessed February 16, 2008.

Pat Fish ("The Jazz Butcher"), Lyrics to "Conspiracy ... Big Questions": http://www.jazzbutcher.com/htdb/lyrics/conspiracy.html.

Nelson Goodman, *Languages of Art* (Indianapolis: Hackett, 1976).

Eduard Hanslick, *On the Musically Beautiful*, trans. Geoffrey Payzant (Indianapolis: Hackett, 1986).

Bennett Reimer, "The Experience of Profundity in Music," *Journal of Aesthetic Education* 29:4 (Winter 1995) 1-21.

R. A. Sharpe, *Philosophy of Music: An Introduction* (Stocksfield: Acumen Publishing, 2004).

Gene Weingarten, "Pearls before Breakfast,"*Washingtonpost.com* http://www.washingtonpost.com/wp-dyn/content/article/2007/04/04/AR2007040401721.html. Accessed April 11, 2007.

INDEX